Marriage and Ministry

How to Have One Without Destroying the Other

By Chris and Linda Padgett

LITTLE RED HOUSE
PUBLISHING

ISBN: 978-0-9990211-3-2

DEDICATION

Linda and Chris would like to dedicate this book to everyone who has ever tried to balance the beauty of marriage and ministry. We are so grateful for you. We also want to dedicate this literary masterpiece to our kids, who really didn't seem to have a choice in whether or not to live this ministry life, but have gone along for the ride nonetheless. Thanks for loving your crazy parents. We want to finally dedicate this book to the many couples who have modeled the beauty of marriage and ministry before our eyes. You impacted us more than you'll ever know. Thank you.

CONTENTS

Introduction

Chris:

Being married, having kids, and doing ministry is like a three-ring circus. We barely get done with one crisis and another one seems to be underway. It is as if we are juggling three balls in the air with life throwing in a few more just to see what happens. With everything that can, and often does, go wrong you would think that we were about to fall apart at any moment, but the opposite is true. We love this crazy circus life! Why? Because we know this is where we get to offer our gifts and talents to one another and the world. This combination of marriage and ministry is our life and we love it. Does this mean that everything is easy or that we never have difficulties? Of course not! What we realized though is that our calling is just that, a calling. Think of the old *Blues Brothers* movie, "We're on a mission from God." Okay, that may not be the best example, but the statement works nonetheless.

I remember one time Linda and I had just returned from West Palm Beach, Florida where I had done a talk in

Lake Worth and visited our old campus, Palm Beach Atlantic College (now University) and on the way home said, "What if we sell our house and move to Steubenville, Ohio?" To which Linda said, "Ok." Ha! To many people, at least at first glance, we appear to be completely crazy. We not only trusted God with where we lived, but with how many kids we would have. In fact, we had so many children that one time a family member mailed an envelope filled with condoms. We have often been misunderstood, overlooked, financially taken advantage of, and hurt by others who knew better, but we pressed on with our family and our ministry as if our life depended on it. And do you know what? It did. Why? Because we knew that God had the best in store for us amidst the difficulties and struggles. There have been a number of moments throughout our marriage and ministry where we thought that maybe a regular job with a steady income would be nice, and then about three seconds later we realize, yeah, that's not going to work.

If you are married and in ministry I am sure you can relate. For those of you who are married and thinking of doing ministry, all I can say is, brace yourself; it will be the most amazing and terrifying ride. What a rush!

Some of you have been doing ministry forever and are about to get married. I just want you to know that so much is about to change, and that's a good thing.

Whether you are in our shoes, or wearing something similar, there are a few tricks of the trade we want to pass along to you. Sometimes it is good to know we are not alone.

As you look at this book I want you to take what works for you and leave the rest. Place yourself into our shoes when it makes sense and recognize when what we are saying isn't a perfect fit. Just as Cinderella was the only one who could fit into that glass slipper, so too, we are the only ones who can live the Padgett ministry experience exactly as we do. We want to help you find your slipper.

I hope you like the book; I loved being yelled at by my wife to fix entire chapters and remember whom the hell I was writing to so that you could hold this in your hands. Truth be told, she is the one who has always made me better, and that may be the greatest tip of all; you are in this together, people, so lean on each other's strengths!

This work is a labor of love from us to you. May the Holy Family encourage you, as you love one another and those put in your path.

Linda:

I knew way back in college that I would marry an evangelist. That's the term used by Protestants to describe a person who travels around telling people about Christ. Back in that Baptist college in the heart of West Palm Beach, I would watch my then boyfriend with his long curly locks put on his "coat of many colors," which was basically his childhood bathrobe that his mother cut off and sewed shut to work as a poncho. This striped terrycloth covering and flip-flops were his "uniform" as he mounted his skateboard and headed off into the dark and scary streets of the inner city. Chris even told me once that he thought he might actually die out there. At least he wasn't being overly dramatic.

Thirty years later, I am not surprised by the fact that we have lived our entire lives together doing ministry. Even as teenagers, there was something built into us that compelled us to serve God as witnesses to his power. Ministry is at the heart of our marriage and family, for better or worse.

Despite the fact that we have always had a united view about the work God has called us to, it has not been an easy road. Marriage is hard, even without the added pressure on time and resources and the spiritual attacks that accompanies the work of God. Marriage and ministry are on their own special callings. A person could use up all their energy keeping either one of these callings afloat. Therefore, a relationship that has combined them together under the same roof is almost equal to Chinese water torture. Why would anyone do that? Why would you put your marriage and family at risk? You are compelled; that's why.

Thanks be to God his grace enough. That's not just a cool Matt Maher song. God's grace is the key to keeping both of these life callings alive.

So, aside from the super juice of Grace, how do you manage a marriage and ministry? How do you have one without destroying the other?

The simple answer is balance. Well, it's not so simple. Obstacles come along presenting serious issue to the scales. Allow Chris and I to share with you the lessons we have learned, not only from our own lives, but also from seeing the number of other couples who didn't manage both, to the grievous loss of one.

#1

Priorities

Chris:

When it comes to Marriage and Ministry, you will not be successful if you don't prioritize the many things that are important.

I remember a friend from a record company who talked about one of his colleagues who was always frazzled and regularly behind. It was as if she moved from one crisis to another. One example he gave dealt with the epic amount of emails she had to "catch" up on. He said, "Whenever I get an email I deal with it right away and immediately delete it when I'm done. I don't let them stack up under the, "I'll get back to them later" file. Address the problem immediately and then move on." I have thought of this advise often, knowing how easy it is at first to place something on the back burner, only to realize later that I am about to get burned because I forgot what was important.

When it comes to marriage and ministry, the most

important priority is to place your marriage first. This is not something that can be pushed back to be addressed later. Your marriage is the place that you gain the graces to be the saint you desire and are called to be. Your marriage cannot be placed on the altar of ministry to be sacrificed for some supposed greater good. The greater good for anyone who is married is to invest and build up your marriage. Over the years there have been many friends who have allowed their marriages to be deeply wounded if not wrecked as a result of their attention on ministry. There is an unhealthy feeling for many that the constant tension, or even sacrifice to do ministry, is somehow virtuous. Here me now: your ministry is not a sacrament; your marriage is. Your ministry is not something that can't be done by another. But, your marriage is something only you can do. No one will be a husband to your wife better than you. No one will be a better wife to her husband than you. Don't allow anyone else to come in and try and take that 'job' from you. Marriage is your first priority, period.

How important is marriage to God? He begins the Bible with a union of our first parents. God likens his relationship to unfaithful Israel as a marriage in the book of Hosea. Jesus begins his public ministry at the Wedding

Feast in Cana. St. Paul talks about the love Jesus has with his Church as a Bride Groom loving the Bride, and the Bible ends with the Wedding Supper of the Lamb in the book of Revelation. God has disclosed himself in Salvation History as a Family: Father, Son, and Holy Spirit. God is Love, and the complete gift of Father to the Son in the love of the Holy Spirit is uniquely expressed in the love of a man and a woman in holy matrimony, open to life.

It is my firm conviction that success in ministry is predicated on the support of a spouse if the leader is married. In other words, the only reason I do ministry is that my wife is all in. It is from this unity, even in the years where Linda never wrote any words to a blog or book, before she spoke publicly, that I was able to give to those I ministered to something beautiful. Why? Because there was no tension from the one I was trying to alleviate in the other. Often what happens in marriage and ministry is that one area becomes a place of tension and a feeling of being misunderstood and under appreciated becomes a foundation of discontent, while the other, in many cases ministry, becomes an almost compliant spouse. Ministry very often can be predicated upon a certain cause and effect, whereas marriage is a relationship with a real person who may be having a difficult day. There are many reasons why priorities get lopsided, and often they are understandable, but to remain indifferent when there is an unbalanced focus is a recipe for disaster.

In order for me to be an effective minister in a authentic ministry, I need to make sure that I am "doing" ministry in my home, with my family and investing in the relationships there. Again, we are able to minister with a greater effectivity when we do so out of a firm foundation in marriage and family. Your marriage and family will be there when you move to a different job, or should be! Your spouse is the one who should have your back, point out weaknesses, work with you on getting better, overcoming hurdles, and addressing setbacks. Together you are stronger than if you try and do ministry on your own.

I have found over the years that I cannot give to those in ministry something authentic and beautiful if I am not growing in my relationships with my wife and family and growing personally.

I love the phrase, you can't give what you don't have. I find it to be so true. If we try and give something that is not intrinsically ourselves to another, we only pretend an authenticity that is not entirely us. What if you imagined you were able to do surgery because you liked the medical community? That does not equate to an ability to actually serve in such a manner. Really, you have to give what you have, in order to truly make a difference. When it comes to marriage and family you need to be entirely yourself. When I am growing in my faith and pouring out to those I love what I am learning, it helps my marriage, and together we are able to be more present and helpful to our family. If I am willing to ask myself difficult questions as to my behavior, individually, maritially, or in my family, then I am able to have victory over struggles and have a true gift to give to those I am ministering to outside of my home.

In ministry situations we value the idea of putting into effect the Great Commission, specifically Judea and the Ends of the Earth, but have somehow minimized the Jerusalem portion. Your family cannot be neglected so that you can go out and minister to others. Start at home and from there you can reach even more than previously imagined.

Linda and I have done a lot to nurture our own

individual faith lives, but it was never meant to be just for us. We want to grow individually in our relationship with Jesus because we desire to know him and share that intimacy with one another. Together, we long to bring the Jesus that we know to our children. Praying together with one another, going to Church or other sacraments, and even speaking words of affirmation and healing are all parts of what it means to minister in our own Jerusalem.

So what do you have to give? You have a spouse that God brought into your life. You have family members who need you to invest time and talents in, and you have a soul that needs to be grounded in regular encounters with a God who loves being with you. If you deny those areas the opportunity to be with Jesus, you will be unable to do for Jesus. First we must *be* so that we can be effective when we do. The doing must flow from being, and that counts when we apply this to marriage and ministry. You and I must be in our marriages so that we can do in our ministries. The priority is marriage, and if you rob that sacrament the opportunity to grow and thrive, what makes you think the success of a ministry counters the death of a marriage?

I understand there are a number of variables that can

make this idea problematic, so this doesn't necessarily hit every possible scenario, but generally speaking I believe this principle of investing in your family first is necessary. For those of you who are having trouble in your marriage, I am begging you to invest in it once again; don't give up if you still have breath to try again. If you are having trouble in ministry, but your spouse and family support you, then rest and know you are going to be okay. The enemy hates people who serve God and advance the Kingdom, but I believe the enemy brings an all-out assault on those who model the love of God in time in the sacrament of marriage. Why? Because when people see a picture of God, it will change how they live and even what they long for.

Linda:

How do you balance marriage and family with ministry? The short answer is YOU DON'T. The scales of balance will never be perfect. Why? Because they shouldn't be. Keeping your life and ambitions in the proper order of priorities is important for success. I am a queen at justifying my disconnect from my spouse and children. Even though I don't leave the house as much as Chris to do the ministry that I have been called to do, doesn't mean that I can't elevate the work over the responsibilities I have with my family. There is always another project that needs completed. There is always another book to write or email to send. My vision and dreams are never ending; therefore, my ambition to get them realized can be overpowering.

Work-a-holics are easy to identify in the regular world. We picture them working late into the evening as the office cleaning staff does their jobs. Their obnoxiously loud phone calls to clients during your son's little league game makes you roll your eyes in disgust. They sit alone at the bar because their obsession with success has driven the possibility of a relationship far from them. However, when it comes to those in ministry, we justify our obsessive behavior because we are doing good work. We're not trying to get rich; we are trying to save souls.

But here's the truth. Our primary vocation is to our spouse and family. Whether you are a man or a woman, whether you have young children or older, whether you get a pay check or not, your marriage and family comes first. There is nothing so important in the work we have to do that is more important than loving those closest to us. Ministry starts in the home, not in spite of it.

As I have struggled with this very issue lately, I hear the voice of God whisper in my ear this question, "What's the worst that could happen?" So what if things are a little late? Is it the end of the world if that project doesn't get completed? In our minds we imagine great failure or problems if we don't complete the things we deem as being so important. But the truth is, God doesn't need projects. He doesn't need books, gigs, events, or any other type of ministry. He needs US. We are the primary instruments he uses. And the context in which he most desires to use us is in our marriage and family. Anybody can lead a youth conference, but no one can parent your children better than you. And the way the kingdom of God is going to grow is by one little soul at a time, starting with those immediately in your charge.

Through our years in ministry, Chris and I have not always gotten this right. We are both pretty driven people. So there are a few safeguards that we have come up with to help keep us focused on the proper priority.

The Heads-Up:

When Chris gets home from a trip, I have come to learn that the two most important things on his mind are garbage and mail. It must be the way he decompresses. He walks around the house picking up all the stray garbage that our messy family has failed to get into the trash. Then he disappears into his office to comb through the pile of mail on his desk. For him, there is a sense of control. Through garbage and mail, he puts his life back together. It acclimates him back into home life. Recognizing this was a huge grace for me. I don't have to fight for his attention or get frustrated by his disappearance right after getting back. I allow him to do his thing. However, after a short amount of time, I give him the Heads-Up. I'll say, "Hey, when you get a moment, I have some things to tell you." For him, that is like a cue that tells him it's time to reemerge. It's hard to fight the temptation to dump on him as soon as he gets in the car. But if I really want to be fully heard and my concerns or thoughts validated, it's best to let him have his reentry time.

Scheduling Fun:

If I don't write fun family activities into my calendar, they simple won't happen. I will allow work and my own driven ambition to take up all of my waking hours. So, just like every other important thing, I schedule fun. The Padgetts like to bowl. So I will look ahead to find the best time for us to go let loose. Of course, I will usually pick a time that the weather is bad, so I don't miss out on good outside project time. The fun doesn't even have to cost anything or make us leave the house. For some reason, the fall ignites something deep inside me that compels me to play video games. My boys love that. It may seem weird that video games are quality family fun, but for us it is. I play all the easy parts and hand over the controls to my kids to battle the big bosses. We all like it that way.

However, even though I may be driven to play, my ministry to-do list is always calling my name and will win out if I allow it. So, Friday evenings have become pizza, wings, and video game family fun night.

Other Interests:

The final safeguard that we have established in our family is developing interests that are not related to ministry. I love DIY (Do It Yourself) projects, biking, BBC, and working on the farm. Ministry cannot be allowed to consume our every moment, conversation, or interest. We need to talk about things other than work. Even though taking on the responsibilities of a farm or DIY projects, or feeding my insatiable appetite for biking, or spending sometimes way too much time watching my beloved British TV just adds more demands on my time and energy, we have found that having these other interests keeps our marriage and family life from becoming stale. Sure, our life is busy, but it's also eclectic. It's interesting. Having multiple areas of interest only adds flavor to your ministry and marriage.

#2

Expectations

Chris:

I was so excited to be presenting in Colorado at a
parish I'd never been to before. Over the years I have had
some wonderful experiences with the diocese of Denver,
and this was going to be a great night sharing the faith.
After finishing my talk I went over to the lady who had
brought me in, just to make sure she loved it; I mean, how
could she not? I was exhausted in a wonderful way,
knowing I had left nothing on the table. I asked her if she
was cool with my talk and I can still remember her saying,
"It was great, but when were you going to talk about
chastity? That's what everyone is here to listen to."
Basically, there were a few moments of awkward silence
until I could come up with a reason I had obviously
deviated from the original plan. I had no idea I was
supposed to do a chastity talk, and apparently she had no
idea that I didn't know that. I had done countless chastity
talks in my life, and in fact, have a book that helps
promote the importance of chastity; I just didn't know that

was what she expected.

This miscommunication and unmet expectations is an important point to talk about when we discuss marriage and ministry. If you don't know how the other person thinks, what their thoughts are on a particular topic, or how they think processing information should go, you are bound to fail. If you don't know their expectations, it is probable you won't meet them; and therefore, you will have fallen short. Clarity in communicating what you want and how you want to get there is imperative for marriage and ministry. I want to press out what your preconceived expectations are in marriage and ministry and examine how we set ourselves up for failure by holding to preconceived and often-unrealistic expectations.

At ministry events, I often ask couples to write on a piece of paper a number between one and ten that bespeaks where they think they are in their relationship with their spouse. Often I will do the same exercise with people concerning their relationship with God. Try it out. What number would you put for your relationship with your spouse? What would you put for your relationship with God? The former is important, because if you put a seven and she puts a one you really need to talk about why there is such a big difference between the two. I tell couples that the number is misleading because we all ebb and flow, and it is almost impossible to have each of you put a ten. You can fluctuate all over the place depending on circumstances, indigestion, or the day. The goal is to try and move one point up with one another, and they can do that by asking how they can improve. By the way, we do this in a very controlled environment so please don't go playing this game with family and friends; it can end horribly. When it comes to huge gaps in the numbers, it is usually because one person's expectations are not being met. They expect their spouse to listen better, help with cleaning, or cooperate with discipline. Maybe they feel like there is little to no romance or quality time is absent, he is too focused on sports or whatever. The expectations not being met can cause a great divide in a relationship and it will not accidentally fix itself. You have to grow in communicating what you expect and work with joy to fulfill and advance in a relationship. It is your job as spouses to bless and meet the expectations of one another.

When it comes to your number with God, this is a very different situation. Your number may be a two or four today, but have you thought about why? Why would you put that number lower today lets say? The reason we put the number lower is based on what we have done or think we should have done. We believe that our disappointment with our performance is something that God shares. This is where we set ourselves up for continued failure, because God does not gauge his love for us based on our performance; rather, the Scriptures say that while we were yet sinners, Christ died for us (see Rom. 5:8). We are loved regardless of what we do. We are loved because he gives the entirety of who he is; and he is love. We are loved not because of an act or action or because we perform or excel; we are loved because he chooses to do so, independent of what we have done. The profound importance is that we are reactionary beings, and when we believe we are loved so entirely, and often so undeservedly, it provides a foundation for a proper response motivated from gratitude and not a hidden desire to gain favor. The relational dynamic between God and us is grounded in the truth that it is always a ten from his perspective. But what do we do with the bad days and sinful moments? He aches for us, I believe that, but it is only because we are robbing ourselves of the opportunity to thrive. We limp instead of sprint. He is not mad that we have sinned; rather, he provided a way to be free from the shackles that enslave and aches for us to avoid what so easily ensnares us.

Lets look at it this way. What does it look like for you to be a great follower of Jesus? A great disciple and, ultimately, a great saint? Or even ministerially, what does it look like to be a great DRE, youth leader, Deacon, or Priest? You have in your mind a checklist of things that if performed make up the job expectations, if met you receive high marks, if not met, you fail. We approach God in the way that we approach job performance or the general decision process of a successful business. But God isn't looking for us to be independent contractors or corporate entities, reducing our worth to a bottom line, or the effectivity of our usefulness. God simply wants to be with us, and the response of being is what should produce the doing. We love God because he first loved us. It is meant to be a reaction. So, if we are not living up to an idealized version of what we think it means to be a saint, spouse, or even a minister, it is either we have a false expectation or we are trying to move before we have *been* with God.

Pursuing an idealized version will exhaust and even destroy a ministry, person, and marriage if it continues.

Why? Because there is little authenticity in it. I know a couple who in many ways were the ideal religious couple. They prayed the Rosary together with their family on a consistent basis, went to Mass, did ministry, and seemed to be perfect. They are divorced now. Do you know why? It wasn't, as far as we know, infidelity or anger issues, drinking or any moral calamity; it was a devotion to ministry over one's devotion to the reality of a broken family life. They wore the mask perfectly. They had it together on the outside, but on the inside, there was a constant effort to perform and act in a certain way, even if it wasn't real.

The problem with pursuing an idealized version of anything is that it has no place in the here and now. The idealized version, or even a comparison with someone else will only set you up for failure, self-loathing, resentment and despair. What does it look like for you to be a saint? To be a great minister? To be a spouse? If that picture in your head doesn't include the reality of your mess, your struggle, and your past, your future will be very unhappy.

So often when we make a mistake and begin to be upset because we are not performing well or according to our idealized expectation, we tend to look at the failure and want to convince God that we know what we have done was wrong and so to prove that, we hold on to the failure extra tight with a laser like focus, trying to prove to God that we are not minimizing how bad that particular blunder was. We make promises and proceed with brutal mental floggings so that God will know that we have not minimized how bad the sin was nor tried to get out of it by just moving on. When we make a mistake we focus on the bump in the road for unreasonably long periods of time instead of moving on and avoiding the next bump we see along the way. If we maintain the idealized version, we focus on the bump as the reminder that we have not achieved perfection. We think that if we try harder now, we will not stumble again, and yet we do. I want to tell you why I think the Lord allows us to continue on like this for long periods of time because there will likely come a time when the idealized version will be so exhausting that we finally declare that we give up. Jesus allows us to continue *trying* to fix ourselves, do things that we think are the perfect spiritual expression so that we will eventually *give up*. Once that happens miracles can take place. God is the only one who can bring the victory we so desperately want. With God all things are possible. Greater is he that is in us than he that is in the world. You see, when we give up, we can finally allow Jesus to come to us in the mess that is our reality. When he ministers to us there, we are grateful. When we are grateful, we are motivated to share, in gratitude, the love we have received to others who so desperately need love. All of ministry, marriage, and spiritual growth have to be grounded in Jesus meeting us in the reality of our now. I am not saying works are bad; rather, I am saying that works motivated by gratitude is what will be life giving and not exhausting.

This principle of allowing God to be in your mess, in the now, destroys the appeal of an idealized version because the God who rescues us in our reality is a God we know others need as well.

I have felt that we offer a Jesus to our parish family that we ourselves do not know. We can't live up to the expectation we are placing on them, and in many ways we perpetuate the problem by pretending this approach is attainable. We need brave ministers and spiritual leaders who will talk about how God met them in their difficulty, mess, and in their normalcy or insecurity because that is the God the congregation most longs for. This idealized version of spirituality must be destroyed. We need real saints who have met a real God who really loves them in the reality of their now. Stop pretending and start letting God love you right where you are. Did you struggle with a sin last night? Did you drink too much, get angry with someone at work, steal, cheat, lie, eat too much, sleep too long, look at pornography, speak about another behind their back, or talk about yourself too much? Did you ignore the hungry around you, despise the needy as you drove past that person with a sign, and promise to pray for the sick but forgot? If you did, welcome to the club. Do we want to stay in these places of struggle and addiction? Of course not. But in that mess, Jesus comes to each of us and ministers to us as the Good Samaritan ministered to the broken man so many others ignored. Jesus is not afraid of your mess, and his love is able to not only minister to you but also give you strength to avoid that which enslaves. The truth is, I am still learning how to let God love me where I am, in all of my insecurities, addiction, and hidden expectations that I clutch so tightly. I too need to rest even more in Jesus, but so often, I wonder if he really will satisfy my need.

This principle of allowing Jesus to meet you in the now is important in marriage because it is something we must model to one another as spouses. When we get married, we may have an idealized version of what we think it will look like, what we think having kids will be like, what we think we will drive, the house we will own, and the job we will have. But when real life hits, we find things to be usually radically different from the idealized version we nurtured so carefully. The reality of life wrecks the idealized versions, and that is a good thing. Loving the real spouse is what you are called to, and the graces given in the sacrament will help you do just that. Part of the problem couples have is that the idealized version of marriage and family isn't met, and they pursue it tenaciously, causing exhaustion and frustration. As a couple, allowing the reality of you as a unit to be entirely what it actually is, is the greatest gift you can give to one another.

Are you exhausted yet? If so, thank God! Finally! God will not force any of us to be authentically ourselves, nor will he coerce or manipulate things so that we give everything to him. There is something at work in this heavenly relationship where Jesus is inviting us to trust him, not just with our successes, but to entrust to him our failings, our expectations, wants, and ultimately, our needs. Trust is never easy, but the way it is *earned* if you will in this situation is that God already proves his love for us in that while we were yet sinners, he died for us. This act is the demonstration that his love is not some hopeful ideal; rather, it is a fact! His love is a fact, demonstrated in a complete gift of self, so that we can look and see and realize that he is worthy of our trust. I know it seems funny to say it that way. Of course he is worthy of our trust, but we only know that in our mind, we have so often failed to realize that in our heart. How do I know? Because of the way we act. We keep trying to convince him to love us, to forgive us, to give us a second, third, or millionth chance. He knows we need a radical reason to entrust our mess, that honest mess with him, and so he takes every sin, every failing and in love destroys its effect and impact on our soul. Now he keeps reaching out for us to place our hand in his and walk in a way we never imagined. In a small way, that moment when Peter gets out of the boat is what it looks like to trust God in our exhaustion. They were exhausted from maneuvering through the storm and terrified at what they thought was a ghost. When Jesus tells Peter to come, he gets out of the boat and does what should never have been possible: walking on water. This is what it looks like to trust God, who sees our exhaustion and our inclination to fear, he calls to us. Will we respond?

And, to make us feel even more confident in this relationship of trust, the next part of the story where Peter takes his eyes off of Jesus and sinks shows us the response of God. Jesus reaches down and simply asks why did you doubt? There is no reproof. For those of you who are sinking and have taken your eyes off of Jesus, he is ready to bring you next to him. Don't doubt his love. He is not inclined to rehash mistakes, especially since the work that is before you is of such importance.

The expectation that God has of us is, I believe, to learn how to let him love us more. This receptivity is our motivation and all that would distract from that love has been addressed at the cross. Sin and fear are no longer worthy adversaries when we trust the one who loved us at our worst, and continues to love us in our now. This moment is your now. Right now he is captivated with you, inviting you to stand next to him. Right now he is asking you to let him into the private areas of your life, the secret past, the broken childhood and dishonest nights. Jesus is worthy of your trust and can breathe new life into dry bones. Is your marriage struggling? Place it honestly into his hands. Is your spiritual life a wreck? Just be with him and hear how much he loves you.

Linda:

If you are in ministry, you have been involved in some event that was dependent upon the weather cooperating. Fall festivals get rained out. Snow cancels a retreat. The main speaker's flight gets delayed due to lightening and can't make it on time. The examples could go on forever, and if you are like me, it makes me scratch my head. After all, we are doing God's work. Doesn't he want the event to succeed? Why can't he make the weather behave?

Expectations. That is what it comes down to. We expect things to go our way because we are doing it God's way. The God of the entire universe, who spoke creation into existence, who formed us in our mother's womb, should be able to make it not rain for a few hours on Saturday. Right? Yet, it doesn't always work that way.

The fact is, God doesn't line circumstances up all nice and neat in order to work; he works despite the messiness. He doesn't need perfection to be successful; he is perfection. All other details fade in comparison to that.

So it is with our marriages and families when involved in ministry. Another major obstacle in the effectiveness of a combined vocation is unrealistic expectations.

Seriously, we are a family who is serving God together, dang it. Life shouldn't be this messy. Our children shouldn't struggle with their faith. Our marriage shouldn't have dry times. Our finances shouldn't be this far below the poverty line.

When it comes to expectations there are two angles I want to talk about. There are the expectations that we have for our family and ourselves, and there are the expectations that we have placed on God.

Our expectations for ourselves:

So many couples only dream about the opportunity to do ministry together. I know many women who would love to have their husbands join them on this venture of a united calling. So the fact that you as a couple have a desire to work together, even if one partner is more of a support system, is a real blessing. Therefore, why in the world should it be so hard? You both want the same thing, why are there arguments? You pray together, your children participate in all of the events, you talk about your faith openly; yet, your marriage and family is far from perfect.

It's important to keep in mind that God uses imperfect people. That's all he has to choose from. All of the perfect ones are hanging out with him in heaven. Since God's options are few, he must make due with you and your imperfect spouse and your imperfect children. Accept the reality of your imperfection. Sure, it may be embarrassing when your child messes up in big ways or one of your teens in your youth group overhear you and your spouse having a very heated discussion. And there is nothing wrong with seeking marriage or family counseling during those rough times. It doesn't make you a failure.

When our teenage daughter informed us that she was pregnant, our world shook. Sure, we were scared for all of the struggles that this unplanned pregnancy would create in her life, but in all honesty, we were scared for ourselves too. We are a couple who does talks on chastity. We live our family's faith life in a very public manner. We knew people didn't think we were perfect, but this messy? This is the kind of mess you want to hide from people, but as with every pregnancy, you can't hide it for long. We discovered who our true friends were. We were told how others were blessed by our response to this news. And in the end, little Audrey has made a lasting impression on our lives, which in turn leaves a lasting impression on our ministry.

By living an imperfect authentic life in front of those to whom you are called to minister may be the most powerful message you can relay. Life is messy. Families are messy. Marriages are messy. But God loves us anyway and desires to bless and use us. Give yourself a break and pass that on to your spouse and family.

Our expectations of God:

Years ago, I heard a preacher say, "If you want to get rich, go into ministry." I remember thinking, "Well, we are doing something seriously wrong."

When Chris and I decided to quit our jobs and go full time into ministry, we were dirt poor. We knew it wasn't going to be an immediate success story of God's rich blessing, but we weren't prepared for the real struggle. Chris spent hours every day making cold calls. He called church after church and tried to convince them to pay the band to minister to their teens. The random booking would send him dancing through the house. Scarecrow & Tinmen played anywhere that would let them, including nature gardens, retirement homes, bookstores, and Home Depot singing Christmas carols. The pay was pathetic, but we were happy.

Once in a while, frustration would build up. I would get tired of not having money to buy the luxury items like ketchup and toilet paper. We would pray and pray for money to show up in the mail so we could pay our extremely overdue car payment or restock the pantry with necessities. Our hearts would jump when we saw an envelope that wasn't a bill, hoping it would contain money. I remember one time I got so excited to see a check because we literally had no food in the house. Yet disappointment struck when I saw that the amount was for only $20. I thought, "Really God?" Twenty bucks can't do much for the grocery needs of our growing family. Why couldn't he send more? But I took the money and marched to the store. I prayed my way through every aisle asking Mary to lead me into making the best choices to feed my family healthy food for such a small amount of money. We survived.

The stories from that time in our life are filled with God's miraculous provisions. They were never over the top. He never sent someone to pay off all our bills or fill our fridge with food. The random twenty dollars in the mail or a few bags of groceries left on our door step were God's way of saying that he was going to take care of us, but we needed to continue to trust.

A life spent in serving God is exciting and difficult. It's easy to assume that because we are doing *His* work, things will go our way. We won't need to go through bankruptcy. Our cars will work when we need them to. Our health will hold out a little longer. But the truth is that a life in ministry is a life of carrying the cross. We must lay down our expectations of how we see God blessing us and our work. We must not allow frustration to overtake us when life gets hard and God seems absent. He's always there. His lessons of trust are one of the greatest gifts he can give you and your family. Learn them well.

#3

Unity

Chris:

I have been with Linda since I was seventeen years
old. It isn't just that we've grown up together, but that we
have grown in all areas of our life together. We have
matured in our spirituality, our bodies and intellect, our
empathy and understanding, to the point where we
regularly acknowledge that we are the same two young
kids that fell in love but are entirely different people. We
have allowed each other to become what we were meant to
be, with a great expectation at what the future holds. In it
all, we have grown together with a freedom and
excitement that is one of the greatest gifts ever given and
received. There has always been a desire to grow old
together, and knowing we were going to do so within the
world of ministry was pretty much a given from those very
early years of dating. How could we be so confident in one
another and our call to ministry? We both knew in our gut
that it was what we were made to do. I know it sounds
crazy to some, but there has always been an understanding

in our relationship that if at any time the path we are on is not the one we want to be on anymore, then we would find a way to either make it work or move to a different path.

The biggest example of radically depending on each other and on God came early in our marriage. Linda was teaching and I was just starting to share my music with a couple people with the hopes of recording and playing a few gigs. What I really wanted to do was be like Keith Green and play the piano for people and talk about God, but somehow I ended up forming a band. The desire to do what I loved was shared by myself and a couple guys, and within a short period, our little group went from being Scarecrow and Tinman (think Simon and Garfunckel) to Scarecrow and Tinmen. We had three people, and our first gig was at the Salvation Army in Sarasota, Florida. We had tracks for synth and drums and got paid $100. Living large! Around that time, my boss was about to fire me because I was horrible at my job, to which I readily agreed and decided to quit before I could be dismissed. It was in this period of me leaving my job that Linda shared her desire to leave teaching, the only steady income we really had. Just as I desired to do what I loved, so did too Linda. She wanted to be home with the children, and in that she supported my mad desire to jump into full time ministry, it was only fitting that I support her jumping into being a stay-at-home mom. We were poor, but happy. That decision to jump into what we both wanted to do changed our lives.

Linda and I have practiced a radical dependence on God's provision amidst seemingly impossible scenarios. Bills needed to be paid, groceries purchased, and family to care for all rested on a ministry that was barely able to pay one person let alone three band mates and their families. We were insane. In it all, Linda and I clung to one another and our desire to love and please God. We began to recognize that we could not out give God in generosity. Every time we tried to sacrifice more, it was as if God one-upped us.

One decision we made early in our marriage was that we would choose together what we would do and would never use the word divorce no matter how difficult times became. We were in it for the long hall. Over the years, it is incredible to realize just how important that unity has been in our success maritally and ministerially. Together we are unstoppable.

When I would travel to venues around the country, people would love to come to the concerts and were often surprised to see my wife and children at the product table after the show. There was an understandable interest in my family; the beautiful wife with kids coming to the show and uniting together in ministry. What they didn't realize is that my wife had spent the last two hours in a small room with numerous kids going bonkers, surviving until they could come out and be adored by countless teens. It was so easy for me to be on stage and such a sacrifice on her part to be with me trying to keep kids quiet until they could finally come out and be with daddy.

Over the years, I would tell people that if they could meet Linda they would realize why anything happens at all in my ministry. She is my shrink, my best friend, my advocate, and warrior, but she is also my heart and, as she would say, my backbone. Linda would believe in our call to ministry when I wondered if I could even go on. It was her support that allowed the band to continue from my end, of that I am sure.

Throughout the early years, we had people try out for band positions, and I would always tell them that to play in our band was a calling. I knew that it would be hard, and I knew that as a ministry there would be difficulties, so they had to be called to it or they wouldn't last. If they were married, I wanted to know what their wives thought about the idea of them joining a band. If there was any hesitancy at all, I didn't want them. I knew that if there were division at home, their time ministering with us would be brief.

You see, ministry has to flow out of a person, but when you are married, that unity and desire to serve must come out of the two that are one, together. In other words, doing ministry when you are married isn't just one person.

Years ago, a youth director told me how he got the job for his diocese. He said that when he met with the bishop and they had finished the interview process, he looked at the bishop and told him, "You know you are going to be getting my wife in the process if you hire me." To which the Bishop nodding with great joy. I love that story. My friend knew he wasn't just getting a job, but was doing a ministry that to be successful in, his wife had to be all in as well.

I can think of another couple who had the perfect relationship on the outside, but their marriage ended because he placed his ministry over his family. She even asked him if he would step down from ministry for a few months to work on their marriage, to which he said no. God does not want you to sacrifice your first vocation on the altar of your ministerial vocation. You must focus on the sacrament if you want your ministry to be successful. I always tell people that the only reason I even do ministry is because Linda is all in. If she were done with me traveling, then I would find a different way to live. Why? Because if I wreck my marriage because of ministry then I have lost it all. What good will it do to have the one and not the other? I would stop ministry to save my marriage. I am sure many people who have had their marriages fall apart would do the same if given another chance.

Trying to juggle family and marriage and ministry is exhausting and a huge hurdle. You are not alone if you feel like you are falling a part. The tips we give at the end of this book will help, but recognize that there are times when you just need to step back and take a big breath and evaluate where you are.

A close friend of mine was in a position where his wife was fully supportive, but his job became an agony even though it was a ministry. The infighting and tension, the odd political moves and office shenanigans just took its toll. He eventually moved to a different diocese and suddenly was blessed unlike anything he'd experience in the previous ten years. It was as if they had been waiting for his gifts and talents for ages, and in fact, they had.

What I want you to realize is that, you and your family may be called to ministry, but that doesn't mean you have to stay in a place that is robbing you of the joy of that ministry. Here is my last story. When I was trying to decide whether to continue with the band or not, I remember having a fear that if I moved on, that somehow I would be out of God's will for my life. A guy I was sitting with began to listen to my frustration and told me something that changed my life. He said, "Chris, it isn't an issue of whether God will bless you if you stay in that ministry or not. He will bless you, as in fact he has been blessing you. It is you that he is blessing. The question is, "Are you supposed to stay in that ministry?" I knew that I was not to stay in that ministry and that while the jump into an unknown ministry was what awaited, somehow seeing that God wanted to bless me, independent of whatever ministry I was in, was a huge consolation.

You, your spouse, and your family, is what God wants to bless. Allowing God to bless you there first, is what will give you the strength to continue in difficulties. Why? Because you are not alone in your efforts and energies. You have a team that is all in, and you being all in for them makes all of the difference. I love it! In the end, when I come home from travels, I don't have to tell my family a story to earn their respect. I don't need to sing a song so that they will listen. I get to just be with them and they with me, and it is where I belong. That's good stuff my friends.

Linda:

Okay, this story may seem odd to some of you, but despite the fact that I was a seventeen-year-old girl when it took place, I am convinced that it was truly God's voice I heard that night.

When Chris and I started dating in high school, we would attend a small charismatic church on Sundays. One evening as the service came to a close, the pastor began his typical altar call. However, that night he wasn't doing the regular "come to the front for salvation" invitation. Instead, he asked anyone to go forward who felt they had a call to the ministry. I was the only one in the entire church who went forward. I clearly remember standing there as the pastor prayed over me and hearing the gentle voice of God in my heart. This is what I felt he said. "Linda, I am not asking you to become a missionary or a traveling evangelist; rather, I need you to be Chris's backbone. He will need your strength for the work I have called him to."

Years later, after the band and solo ministry was well underway, I remembered that moment. It was like a light bulb went on in my head, and I saw what the Lord had revealed so many years previous. I knew that my work in ministry was primarily in the role of support. I also knew that the importance of that role was equal to the work God had called Chris to. Never have I been jealous of his calling. Never have I felt insignificant in my role. I am certain that it is this unity in our calling, even though our calls are different, that has provided us the success and satisfaction throughout the years in ministry.

Now, as these role are adjusting to the new dynamics in our family and a more public expression of ministry for me, it is beautiful to see how those years spent in the background were not *wasted*; rather they were used in building the foundation for the bigger, more difficult work the Lord is calling me to.

Unity is something that comes easy for Chris and me. I think it has to do with the fact that we were just kids when we started dating and have held onto that youthful idealism of "us against the world." We know that when we are joined in a common mission, we are unstoppable. Our best qualities make up for the weaker qualities in the other. We love being together, and life doesn't make sense outside of the context of our relationship.

However, through the years, we have seen the incredible destruction that can come about to a family when unity is not present. It's a true tragedy to witness a marriage rip apart because of ministry, not infidelity or lack of communication or "falling out of love," but doing the work of God. It may seem that it's impossibility for something so positive and good to do so much damage, but it often does when a wedge has been driven between the couple.

We've been asked on several occasions about how to deal with a spouse who is not supportive of their work in the church. Our usual advice is to step away from it. God doesn't need you, but your spouse and family does. They are your primary vocation and if you loose sight of that, you will flounder in your other vocations. But if you are looking to bring about a united vision or strengthen the one you have, there are four points I would have you consider.

Communicate:

The two of you have to talk. Assumption is a dangerous thing. Most of Chris and my disagreements stem from us assuming things of the other. Even though you may feel like you have shared your heart about your work in ministry a million times, do it again. However, be careful to not communicate your passion and desire in a way that makes it sound superior to your spouse's work or call. Knowledge and truth give freedom. Even though you may still come to the conclusion that your calls are different, it's incredibly freeing to know and understand each other's heart.

Set expectations:

Throughout the years, it became obvious that Chris could use my help in some organizational way. He would have greatly benefited from my structure and planning. There were times that he even asked for that help. Yet, the reality of our family life and the responsibilities I held in the day-to-day running of that life made it impossible for me to be of any great assistance to him. It would have been unfair of Chris to expect me to do more. He respected the work I was busy doing. In the same way, I couldn't expect him to be the version of a father who went to every sporting event or spent his days building a tree house in the back yard. His work and gifts were different. Sure, spending most weekends year after year alone, while other families were having huge Sunday dinners or going camping or going to the beach together, was, and is, a cross I bear; it is the cross I have chosen to bear. It is just part of our joint calling. Therefore, the expectation we place on each other must match the mission we have put on our lives.

Encourage each other:

Be each other's greatest cheerleader. That is an important element in any marriage, but how much more important is it in a marriage where ministry is a part. We all know that doing the work of God opens you up to attack, not just from the spiritual side, but also from the human side. Allowing each other to vent and express frustrations or discouragement is crucial. We all gravitate toward the biggest sources of positive attention in our lives, so make sure it's you that is that source for your spouse.

Keep the common call in sight:

Like I said, a life in ministry brings with it crosses. Difficult times are bound to visit you. In order to keep unified during those times, you must keep your common call in sight. I have so many memories of kneeling beside the bed of a sick child throughout the long night being the only adult in the house. These were the days before cell phones. I had no way of getting ahold of Chris. Yet, I felt united to him through the joint calling we were living. I knew that despite the physical distance between us, the Lord kept the connection alive. We were in this thing called life and ministry together, no matter what junk came at us.

Wherever you are in your marriage and ministry, find a way to build and preserve unity. It really is you two against the world.

#4

Spiritual

Warfare

Chris:

There is an adversary. I know this is not going to be popular, but you need to remember that not only is God real but the enemy and his efforts at destroying the Kingdom of God are real. We have some basic things to give us confidence in battling the Adversary such as the victory of the cross and the intercession of the Angels and Saints. But also, we know that the gates of hell will not prevail against the Church. Man, have those gates been shaking in a terrifying way as of late. The enemy, Satan, is a liar and, in fact, the father of lies. His whole existence is to try and make a mockery of God's tenacious love for a people that are so often inclined to wrecking themselves. Such an ungrateful lot this human race is, and it is as if the devil derives pleasure at our failings and repeated downfalls. You could easily argue that the enemy hates women because they remind him of the Blessed Mother, and we know from Scripture (Gen. 3:15) that the Woman and her Seed will crush the head of the Serpent. Obviously the devil knows he can't win the war, but he will take as many souls to hell with him as possible.

Those called into ministry need to be aware of the Spiritual Warfare that we are constantly waging, because we are fighting for actual souls. When it comes to the things Christians struggle with, the traditional pillars are the world, the flesh, and the devil. I will be focusing on the devil, but you need to know that his reach is seen in the world, and he tries to rob you of the beauty of your body and its gift. We will explore a little about spiritual warfare here, but remember our God is greater no matter how great the attacks of the enemy appear.

When you get married, the enemy has a greater desire to destroy you than ever before. A holy marriage is a witness of the love God has for his people. Jesus as the Bridegroom and we as the Bride is the example St. Paul gives. So, one of the major attacks from Satan is to try and destroy marriages. Not only does the enemy bring division and resentment, and a number of other tactics to the battlefield that is your marriage, but he also attempts to change what marriage actually is culturally speaking. So, don't be surprised that the definitions of marriage and family are constantly modifying and becoming almost unrecognizable. The enemy wants confusion. Anytime there is confusion, you can assume that there are spiritual forces at work. Consider the Holy Family. How much do you think the devil wants families to model that? It bespeaks the love of the Trinity, and it was the place where Jesus called home, served and loved. When our families are attacked by the enemy, it is so obvious that he wants to rob us of peace. Divisions, arguments, accusations, and any number of tactics are implemented by the enemy to try and rob families of a witness to a world stuck in darkness.

When you find out that you are going to have a baby I believe the enemy has an even greater desire to rob you of peace and brings an all out attack on you. Why? Because that baby bespeaks new life, new opportunities, a new soul for God to love, a new reflection of God's image and likeness to a world in need of healing, and a new saint. So, the lies of the devil permeate the culture and invite people to destroy the baby in utero. Any time you see conflicts in a marriage and family it is probable that the enemy is at work.

Another area that we can see the adversary bringing a greater attack on an individual is when they choose to do ministry. You are decidedly trying to take souls from him. The call of every Christian is to go into all the world and preach the Gospel. This opposition from the enemy in bringing about the Great Commission is nothing new. The early Church encountered a lot of opposition, but the Holy Spirit working in these now empowered men, were able to battle any difficulty and obstacle, whether it be natural (storms), physical (language barriers), internal (missionary difficulties and dietary responsibilities), and supernatural (spiritual warfare with demonic), and even religious (Jews, Gentiles, Romans). In every difficulty, the Holy Spirit gave the missionary Church a way to preach the Gospel. When marriage and ministry is united, there will be an increase in battle to which most people can't compare. Hell has been irritated at every level. You are not just being looked at; you are being strategized against!!!!!

So what do we do? Don't listen to the enemy. God loves you when you fall and he is not giving up on any of us. Apologize to family and friends where needed and realize you are doing something right! You have created a stir in a hornet's nest, just make sure you have yourself ready for the battle.

Battle Tips:

1. Pray. You need to pray more than ever before. Pray with your family, by yourself, with your kids, in the car, as you go to sleep, in the shower, as you speak and think. Pray. It is a constant reminder that you need Jesus. And, my friends, you need Jesus.

2. Grace. Get graces into your life. Prayer is one way; the second is Sacraments. Go to confession often, mass, and remember that marriage is an actual sacrament. You get graces there, but the key to unlocking those graces is to attack problems together. Don't let the enemy divide you as a couple. Be united in your approach to fighting the enemy.

3. Put on the Armor of God: Read that passage in Ephesians and recognize that there are ways to suit up for the battle. Helmet of salvation, feet shod with the Gospel of peace, the Sword of the Spirit (that's a good one), the breastplate of salvation. Look, God wants you to know that you will win. How so? Think of David and Goliath. That story is your opportunity to know that while your adversary may be great and legendary, with God you will win, but you have got to throw the

stone, my friends.

4. Bless. Bless your family often. Pray over each other. Do the sign of the cross upon your families foreheads. Speak life into your children. Remind them that they are yours and you are theirs.

5. Finally, remember that the Devil plays dirty. There is nothing fair about the way the enemy attacks. He will find your weakness and come after it. The people you care about will go through things you have been trying to keep them from experiencing. The enemy doesn't care about you or anyone you love and is not playing by any rules when the attacks begin. He will bring betrayal, people who will scourge and mock you, friends will deny you, and you will feel abandoned, and how do I know all of this? You know the answer. We are all called to take up our cross daily, but keep in mind that those who followed Jesus all were martyred save John the Beloved. The odds are favorable that you will die giving the faith to others. That my friend is some great company to be in.

In the end, the Devil is not hiding behind every bushel, nor is every problem a demon waiting to pounce. The rain falls on the just and unjust; in other words, life happens to everyone. How we respond to circumstances is a big opportunity to live the light in a way that points people to God. That being said, there is a strategy the enemy has to destroy you. Be aware of why you act a certain way, how you respond to failures, how you act to your family when you are hurting. Keep a journal and start thinking like a captain or general for that matter who is about to enter a battle. Ask for the intercession of the Angels and Saints. You are not alone. I am cheering you on, my friends. God may call the most needy people to follow him, because usually we know how much we would fail without him. This will serve you well in spiritual warfare because pride will unhinge a person like nothing else. Knowing you need Jesus is going to be key to victory. Remember when Jesus battled the enemy, he quoted Scripture. He knew his Father, and he didn't allow the appetites to rob him of who he was and is. He didn't let a want satisfy a need. Look at the story of Job. God allowed the enemy to tempt him because he knew that his servant would remain faithful. Wow. You are not alone, friends. We love you.

Linda:

The truth is, Chris and I started doing ministry together way back in college. Even though it was usually Chris and our older, tougher friend John who went into the dark streets of downtown West Palm Beach, I would join them occasionally on various "witnessing" outings. We would find the local hangouts where the teens would park their low riding cars, open their trucks to reveal the massive speakers, and blare their music as they drank, smoked, and did who knows what else. The three of us would wander through the crowds looking for an opportunity to strike up a conversation about Jesus.

A favorite such place that John would take us to for sharing the Gospel was the "strip" in Ft. Lauderdale. This beach side strip of road, filled with bars, live music, and tourist attractions, was a popular location for young people to hang out and engage in all sorts of illegal activity. Being that I didn't even weigh 100 pounds and looked like a pre-teen, the boys always kept me close because it was actually a pretty dangerous place to be by yourself. It was on once such night of witnessing that I came face to face with the dark side of the spiritual world.

Even Christians sometimes forget that there are unseen enemies whose goal is to bring about our destruction. Too often demons and devils are reserved for movies or video games. However, the fact is that this dark spiritual side is ever present and can be seen actively working its evil in our lives, the lives of our family, and the ministry into which we are pouring our hearts.

That night in Ft. Lauderdale has left a permanent mark on my mind. We had seen a group of teens hanging out around a bench so our threesome approached them. They were not hostile towards us. They were looking to have a good time and saw carrying on a conversation with three religious freaks as part of that. I can still see his face. There was a young man, probably an older teen, who seemed to be the leader of the group. During our chat, for a few brief moments, I made eye contact with him. A shiver ran down my spine because it was very clear to me that I was not looking at the person in front of me; rather, there was another presence present. John and Chris felt it too and we decided to move on. John knew we didn't have the strength to deal with that kind of adversary that night.

During our average day in ministry, we don't usually encounter the enemy so blatantly. Unless your work is in the dark trenches of the street or occult, demonic possession is extremely rare. However, the workmanship of evil can be seen and should be expected when God's work is being done. Therefore, if you have decided to mix the important work of the Kingdom with having a marriage and family, it's imperative to be on guard to these workings of evil.

This last year, as Chris and I have embarked on expanding our ministry and forming the new non-prophet, Catholic FAM, we have felt the attacks of the enemy like never before. There have been moments that have left us wondering if we are cut out for this level of battle. The enemy never plays fair. He will always go after our weakest point, and to many of us, that's our family. Like any good sadistic bad guy, manipulating the target by harming their loved ones is a very effective tactic. Sure, it's hard to bear up under the weight of a personal spiritual attack, but to see your children under fire can make you crazy. "LEAVE THEM ALONE!" is what you want to yell. But what I have found is there are two important steps to help protect yourself and your family from the destruction of spiritual warfare.

Pray for protection:

Whether you are husband, wife, father, or mother, God has put you in a position of authority within your family. With that authority comes influence, influence over the spiritual well being of those in your reach. Use that influence. Use that authority.

The prayers you pray for the protection of you family carry an added weight. It's not just like anyone praying for them because you are the gatekeeper. Tapping into that power when you pray will add an extra oomph to your prayer.

"Therefore I tell you, whatever you ask for in prayer, believe that you have received it, and it will be yours." Mark 11:24

Another piece to this authority given to you by God is the right to bless your family. Praying for them is great; however, the scriptures are filled with blessings. We see over and over how parents blessed their children. Because you are a faithful Catholic, you participate in the priesthood of Christ. Therefore, like a priest, you can and should bless your spouse and children.

In our family, this has been practiced since the early days of being Catholic. Sometimes after family prayer, Chris will have the children come up for a blessing from both of us. When I put my young children into bed, I would bless them by making the sign of the cross on their foreheads and say, "May the Lord bless you and protect you, and may he be in your heart forever."

These practices may seem small and insignificant, but like every other spiritual exercises, the real strength of it goes unseen. They require faith.

Enlist the prayers of others:

Even though your prayers of protection for your family carry the greatest weight, it is important to enlist the prayers of others. I have done this through the years in two ways.

The first help I have called upon is that of the saints. When something specific is troubling me about one of my family members, I reach for a novena. There are tons of novenas to choose from, so I search till I find the one that is most applicable. Relics have also been a massive blessing in our family. I don't know how we got so lucky, but we have about a dozen first class relics in our house. At various times of prayer, we have brought them out and kissed them, making a deeper connection with those saints. Even though saints have been given special permission to be present in the lives of us here on earth, having a part of their physical person in our home has had added power to their workings in our lives.

The second way in which I have enlisted the prayers of others is by enrolling my children, and now my grandchildren, into religious orders. No, I'm not having them sized up for habits; rather, I submit their names to be added to the perpetual prayer list of various orders. The Passionists and the Marians of the Immaculate Conception have been the two primary orders I have remained in contact with. When I first did this, I signed up my oldest children through an order who committed to pray for them for fifteen years. I remember feeling a bit of a relief knowing that there would be some holy men and women praying for them for so long. It blows my mind to think that I need to renew this now. Those young babes are now adults and could still use the prayers of these priests and sisters.

For me, the benefit of enlisting the prayers of others brings peace of mind. I grow weary. I get distracted. I simply forget to pray for my family. Knowing that there is someone else out there, either in Heaven or on earth, praying for my family has been a huge blessing to me.

"Prayer is our greatest weapon against evil." This is true. We can do all the right things to protect our families and ourselves against the attacks of the enemy, but when it comes down to it, the best thing we can do is pray.

#5

Sin

Chris:

I have a vivid memory of when I was a little boy, walking down the isle of a Nazarene church in Valley City, North Dakota. I didn't have a heightened awareness of any particular sin, outside of being a little naughty now and then, but I knew that Jesus wanted me to give my life to him. How did I know this? My mother. She told me regularly about how much Jesus loved us and that being in a relationship with him was an important opportunity. Somehow my mother got through my brain that there would be a time that he would call me and I would want to respond. That day, as a little boy, my heart began to beat so loud and fast when the music minister began to sing, "Just As I Am." The pastor invited anyone who wanted to give their life to Jesus that day to get up out of their seat and come down the aisle and accept him into their heart as their personal Lord and Savior. It took some coaxing from the Holy Spirit and a miraculous dose of courage, but I finally rocked myself out of that pew and made my way down to the front of the church. I knelt by the carpeted steps leading up to the pulpit and can remember thinking, "What do I do now?" I just knew that God had called and I responded. Later that year, I agreed to be baptized. That is what people did who had Jesus as their Savior. But Savior from what? I was not entirely sure I could have told you when I was little. I did know that Jesus was real and that he wanted me to be in a relationship with him, but I wasn't aware of any big sins.

When I got into my middle school and teen years, I struggled a lot with sinful things and the reality of what it meant to still try and be in a relationship with Jesus. In the denomination I was a part of, the threat of the Rapture was never far away. I was always in a state of panic when it came to my spiritual condition because I expected that Jesus would take his faithful followers away in the Rapture, and I would be left with all the horrible sinners and Catholics, as the Devil was basically given free reign on earth. I knew I was struggling with a lot of sin and there was no way Jesus was going to want to take me up and stink up Heaven with my mess. So, I must have given my life to Jesus dozens of times in those years. Altar calls, invitations to recommit, you name it I did it. Something must not have stuck when I made that journey to the front of the Church so long ago, because I was certainly not living a perfect Christian life.

The end of my senior year, I was a wreck. I was doing a little drugs, sleeping with my girlfriend, and looking into the occult. I was unhappy, divided, living in the world and feeling unworthy of forgiveness. I was cutting myself a little and thought I had gone too far for God to want me back. In this time of darkness, I was invited to go with friends up to Gainesville, Florida, to get a free electric guitar. I was pumped about that, and once I was there, with guitar in hand I was invited to a bible study that changed my life. There was a minister at the house, and he asked me if I'd ever given my life to Jesus. Ha! I looked at him and decided to be honest. I told him, "Which time?" I don't think he realized the impact of that response, but he didn't seem to care that I was a mess. That night this minister prayed over each person there and Jesus spoke to me. I was half expecting to have a demon manifest itself out of me and the minister suddenly having to do a deliverance service over me as he wrestled with Legion. So, you can imagine the delight as he prayed over me and Jesus whispering in my ear two things he wanted me to do as I took his hand and accepted this massive "second chance." I can remember thinking as the preacher came to me, and even saying to the Lord, "Jesus if you'll take me back I will spend the rest of my life living for you." The Lord told me to go home and apologize to my mother and to my girlfriend. I did, and with Linda it was the beginning of a whole new way of being in a relationship.

What does this have to do with sin? Simple. When I was young, I didn't understand the divisiveness and impact of sin, nor did I understand the way the enemy would use sin to rob me of joy and peace. I didn't know the power of self-loathing, regret, feelings of unworthiness, and I had no way of knowing just how powerful and long lasting bad choices could be. I didn't know how much I needed a Savior. After years of becoming an expert in sin and selfishness, of almost learning how to be divided in one person, how to hate one part of me and tolerate another, I realized that I was defeated. I was so broken.

After that period of inviting God into my life, I went all out in my devotion to Jesus. I prayed all of the time, spent time memorizing the Bible, talking to others about a God of second and third and infinite chances, and knew that I had been given a miracle in coming back to God.

The problem was that I wrestled with that past and that old man so often that I got even stricter and regimented, thinking I could discipline the sinful man right out of me. I prayed longer, studied harder, read more spiritual books, and talked about the faith. I still had this part of me that wanted to be fed, to be given free reign again. I was getting tired and unable to win every battle. I learned how to be legalistic, and became even unhappier. I have a vivid memory in that time of my life where I was so exhausted and unhappy that I stood in an empty basketball court and stared up into heaven with a desperation and ache. What now? I can remember saying to Jesus, "I can't convince you to love me. It will never be enough. I will never be able to do enough to make up for my past, and I will never be able to win every battle. If you won't love me I'm lost." It was one of the most real prayers of my life. It was in this time that the Lord brought a man into my life who convinced me that Jesus liked to be with me. Yes he loved me, but he also liked to be with me. The miracle of this word and this man at that time can never be minimized.

Sin makes us myopic. Sin makes us focus on what we have done and what we haven't done. Sin keeps us from looking around and seeing those who are in need. Why?

Because sin focuses the individual on their unworthiness, their propensity to miss the mark, and the inclination to be defeated. The realization that we are unable to fix that part of our life may take some time, but when it hits, some people give up completely on even trying to modify their desires and become addicted to numerous vices. Other people become so legalistically regimented they are no longer human. There must be a real solution to the reality that is called sin. The solution is a Person. The relationship with this Person is the victory over sin. Let's take a quick look at where we came from and where we can go with this Person.

In the beginning, God created Adam, and Adam had the responsibility to tend and keep this gift. All was gift to Adam. He was given favor to name and care for what God had created. What a wonderful opportunity and responsibility. Adam is lonely and needs communion and so God gives to him Eve. They are in love, truly made for one another. He shares with her all that he has done, all that he has and all that a relationship with God is about. He is free from worry and concern because God has provided all. One tree in the world is off limits, and to ensure Eve knows how serious this tree is to avoid he tells her you can't eat from it or even look upon it. That is a bit of a change from what God told Adam by the way. The question could be asked, why would God place a tree in the Garden that Adam shouldn't eat from? Because love has to be a free choice, and Adam needed to freely choose God for the relationship to be real from Adam's perspective.

In comes the Serpent and he seduces Eve. She eats the fruit. Where is Adam when this is taking place? Standing next to Eve. He says nothing. Some posit that the serpent subtly threatens Adam in that temptation when he says that you will not die if you eat the fruit, almost implying that if they didn't eat the fruit they would die because the Serpent would kill them. The serpent is also known to be a dragon—the great dragon of old according to Revelation. In that moment, this period of testing, Adam is not heroic, and as a result, they are cast from the Garden. We know that the mercy of God is present in the hope of the coming woman and her son crushing the head of the Serpent, but the sin was so severe everything changed. So, why would God put the serpent in the garden if he were such a conniving and seductive creature? Why would God not defend and keep them from such an adversary? The answer is that he provided a way for Adam to obtain victory but he stood there doing nothing. Adam was empowered and equipped to defend and keep that garden. He dropped the ball. Adam not only allowed the serpent into the garden, he allowed fear to influence his inactivity. Remember, perfect love casts out fear, and it is obvious he was not allowing his relationship with God to influence his actions in defending his bride and fighting the adversary.

So, this original sin is now passed on to all of us. Why? Because it is so severe. A temporal creature has offended an eternal being. There is no way to remedy the offense because even if Adam lived a perfect life that is what he was created to do. There is no way to eliminate the offense by doing what one was created to do. What was needed was a temporal being who would live in obedience to God's will, fight the lie of the Serpent and offer eternally the sacrifice worthy of making remedy for the offense to an eternal being. The son foretold in Gen. 3:15 is the only one who can do this. Jesus fights for his bride, he tends and keeps and wages war on the Serpent of old. He fights to the death for the one he loves, and the mortal blow remedies the past and ushers all of us, enslaved by the old Adam to be given a new way of living.

The Last Adam changes everything about the impact of sin.

So, now when we struggle with the world, the flesh, and the devil, we can battle all with confidence because we have been loved by God so decisively that fear is able to be removed from the equation. The problem is that the Serpent still hisses and whispers to everyone, wanting us to focus on our failures and inabilities. Death where is your victory? Where is your sting? In the relationship we have with Jesus, we are invited to do what Adam didn't do. We can tend and keep what God has given to us, and we can fight the enemy with confidence because Jesus has already won the battle and called us to be in Him. In other words, we are the recipients of Jesus' victory over the enemy. So, if we try in our own strength to fight sin and temptation, the devil, and his lies, we will fail, but if we see ourselves in Christ, via baptism, we now have an arsenal of opportunity to see our victory and ability to battle and win. Think of St. Paul writing to the Ephesians where he talks about the armor of God. Think of the gift of being the recipient of every spiritual blessing in Christ (again see Ephesians). We have also received the very Spirit of God that will give us courage to live and share the

Gospel.

Sin tries to rob us of our glory story. Sin tries to tell us that we are not changed that we are no longer lovable. Sin tries to tell us that we cannot endure saying no to our flesh. But God invites us to believe that the story of the resurrection is our story. We have been saved, are being saved, and will be saved by a God who has set us up for success.

Imagine you are a water bottle. I know that's weird, but just pretend. The water bottle is made to hold water. When it is new, it is filled and sealed with a cap to ensure that the water is fresh. That is us at baptism. We are filled with what we were made to be filled with, which is grace. We are sealed by the Holy Spirit. Now, remember Original Sin? For us, we are born with what is called Original Sin, which means we are born with a depravation of grace. We lack grace. When we are baptized, we are filled with grace and sealed by the Spirit and ready to go into this world and live a life of love and faith. But as you know, life can be difficult and we lose grace in a variety of ways. When we lose enough grace we feel empty. When we feel empty, we try to find ways to fill and satisfy ourselves. The problem becomes evident in the various ways people try and fill themselves because so often they try to satisfy their need by pursuing wants. We want to feel loved and accepted and so enter unhealthy relationships. We want to avoid suffering and struggles so we eat and drink excessively or remain unmoved for fear of being hurt. When we choose to try and fill ourselves with something that is not what we need (in this case we need grace), we add to the bottle that is our life something that changes the consistency of what and who we are to be. So, if I add coffee to water the color changes and the taste too. This isn't poisonous but not what the bottle was made to hold. This is what we call Venial Sin and its impact. If I added poison to the bottle it would kills whoever drank from it. This is Mortal Sin, which kills the life of grace within the person. In all cases they are truly filled, but with something that hurts or destroys. God wants us to learn how to be satisfied with him—to be filled by Him. We were made to be filled with grace, and when we lack grace, we are not fully thriving and living the Abundant Life. The question again could be, "Why would the Lord allow for us the possibility of sinning?" Because, as we have seen, love needs to have a free ascent of the will to be authentic. God isn't looking for robots; he is looking to be in a relationship with us, and if we will allow it, he can truly satisfy our greatest desires.

Freedom important, and we are meant to be a witness and reflection of our elder brother: Jesus Christ. We, like Peter, are meant to carry our cross and follow the example of Jesus in becoming a gift for others to know and love God more. When we die to selfishness, it isn't that God loves us more; it is that God's love can shine through us more easily. Why is that important? Because God invites us to be co-laborers with him, to share the Good News (remember the Great Commission?) so that the lost could be found.

Maybe you know all of this, but I am confident that many have not meditated upon these principles. How do I know? Because St. Peter tells us something in his Second Letter that is proof positive for all who have struggled with being ineffective in our ministry or even feeling blind at times spiritually. Peter says that the reason we are blind and ineffective is because we have forgotten we have been forgiven of our past sins. This verse is so powerful because it speaks to each of us who have possibly allowed the story of the cross to be less real and focused on than maybe we intended. After all, we have heard the story countless times and there are crucifixes everywhere in our Church, Catholic Schools, on our Rosaries, and probably in our very homes. St. Paul echoes the importance of the cross to the Galatians when he talks about being crucified with Christ, and he says to the Corinthians that he determined to know nothing among them except Jesus Christ and him crucified. Why? Because when we focus on the cross, we are looking at what total relational love looks like. The cross is where Jesus took every offense to God, past, present, and future and destroyed its impact. Jesus loved us so much that he wanted to free us from the enslavement of sin and offer us a new way of living. Jesus heals our wounds and invites us into the dance of an intimate relationship with God. Imagery of a vine and branches or of a body with its head are all attempts to show that the way God wants to be with us, in us, and work through us is far greater than rote memory or blind allegiance. Jesus wants to love us and show us the beauty of a new way of living.

What if you have yet to actually be fully yourself? I know that is an odd question, but what if the enemy has plotted every moment of your life in such a way as to attack the very opportunities in which you could thrive. He whispers your unworthiness when you hear of God's calling unlikely candidates to ministry. The enemy reminds you of your past and your sins to keep you from speaking with boldness and confidence. The enemy tells you that you can't change the generational sins that you will only get worse, or you will inevitably drop the ball like you always do when the pressure is on. The enemy speaks death into your life so that you will wait in fear. God on the other hand, wants you to focus on perfect love, the perfect love that he has demonstrated to you. The more you focus on that perfect love, the fear begins to leave. God's love is the great motivation to courageously step out into the seemingly unknown and do something insane. Why? Because while the world may see you as nuts, you know that your courageous step is with one hand held by Jesus and the other by Mary. Sin will only keep you from truly living. God wanted you to be free from that paralysis. Let your eyes be fixed on Jesus, the author and perfector of your faith. He is inviting you to live in a way that the world will find both amazing and impossible. Be the exception to the rule. Be the witness of a new way of living. Be his and realize that you can do all things in Christ! It is okay to be needy. Did you know that? God is not afraid that you need him to remind you of how much you are worth. God is not upset when you stumble and hobble back onto his lap. He has always loved you. He has always wanted to spend time with you. He actually likes you.

Linda:

Do you remember Michael English? I was obsessed with him and his music back in the early 90's. I can't listen to the song, "Mary did you know" without thinking of him. He was the first artist to record that now over-used theologically incorrect song. My little world shook when the news broke of his infidelity, and his career never fully recovered.

When sin takes root in the life of someone in ministry, the effects can be far reaching, even to a young girl in Florida. However, when that person also has a marriage and family, the results can be devastating. No one, not one single person doing the work of God plans on ruining his or her life.

This obstacle in balancing marriage and ministry is the one to keep a close eye on. Sin has a way of sneaking up on us. Small dishonesties, bad choices, and lack of accountability is the perfect recipe for the disastrous storm of wreck and ruin.

The sin that can cause this kind of mess doesn't have
to be just a sexual sin. Even though infidelity and
pornography are two of the most common, the sins of
pride, greed, envy, and dishonesty can be just as
damaging. An individual's pride can easily sway the scales
of balance out of whack. Being consumed with success or
acceptance draws our attention away from the love and
acceptance of our family. Being driven by money (greed)
or being absorbed by dissatisfaction with your life (envy)
are ultimately selfish concerns, which, in turn, puts you
out of balance with both your family and your ministry.

Thanks be to God that in the twenty-three plus years of
full-time ministry, Chris and I have managed to avoid the
devastating outcome of serious sin. Yes, we do sin. Yes,
we have to maneuver through the land mines of
imperfection; however, we have been blessed to have had
set down important boundaries and practices that have
kept us free from the big sin issues.

When I take a long hard look at the ways we have
managed to keep sin at bay during these years of ministry,
I can separate them into two main areas: secrets and

intimacy.

No Secrets:

This is a huge rule and practice for us. We didn't sit down one day and discuss the importance of not keeping secrets from each other; we just have always done this. We started dating as a couple of crazy seventeen-year-olds. We didn't know any better. We told each other everything, no matter how hard or embarrassing, and we've never stopped.

No joking, I have seen couples who lie about how much they spent at a garage sale. Seriously? The table only cost $25, why would you say it cost $15? Is that $10 worth the integrity of your relationship?

Even on big issues, Chris and I have kept the lines of communication clean, not muddied with dishonesties. One such time was years ago when I was working full time as a kindergarten teacher. For some reason, as I was getting ready in the morning, I noticed that I was becoming concerned with the way I looked and wondered if my boss found me attractive. I have no idea where this came from. I had absolutely no attraction for him. I am sure the feeling was mutual. It was just these little random snippets of thoughts. This went on for a couple weeks and I became pretty frustrated with them. Did they make me a bad person? Was I sinning in some way? I never invited this line of thinking in myself. One day, I decided to tell Chris about them. I was ashamed of these thoughts and was concerned that he would be upset at me. However, I knew, like really knew deep down, that I needed to tell Chris. I felt that these thoughts were originating in a dark place and I needed to shine some light on them. Being honest with my husband was the best way to do that. So, I told Chris. His response was basically a shoulder shrug. He thought my concerns were silly and knew that sometimes thoughts pop into our heads and it doesn't mean we have done something immoral. I felt immense relief. And, do you know what? I never had another thought like that again. Poof. Gone.

The family saying that has come out of this experience is this: Secret sin leads to more secret sin. As long as a sin or near occasion of sin is kept under the cloak of a secret, it has power and will only continue to grow stronger. The best way to nip it in the bud is to bring it to the light.

Sure, some of these things can be hard to talk about or

embarrassing, but once they are revealed, the strength to overcome any temptation that may accompany them will be gained.

Work On Intimacy:

Chris travels almost every weekend and has done so for the last twenty-three years. When he's home, our large family demands a lot from us. Sporting events, doctor's appointments, chores, shopping, homework, church… the list could go on and on. Intimacy is the area in our lives that can easily be overlooked for more pressing things like survival.

The intimacy between a husband and wife is the grounding conduit for a family. All hell could be breaking loose, but if mom and dad still love each other and actually act like it, the structure of the home stays intact. The same is with ministry. Even though God thankfully uses broken people all the time, there is something stable and empowering about a ministry that has the strength of an intimate marriage behind it.

For Chris and I, intimacy gets worked on in several different ways. Spending time together is key. Since we are apart for such long periods of time, when Chris is home, we do almost everything together. It's rare for us to become preoccupied with separate interests. If I want to bike, Chris will bike with me. If Chris wants to go on the hunt for more books that won't fit in our house, I will go with him. Date nights have always been a part of our marriage. Thank God our children are now old enough to watch each other.

Talking is the other way we build intimacy. We are crazy dreamers. We love to talk about our goals and ambitions. One of my favorite activities is to go for a walk and chat. Chris is my best friend. There is no one I want to share the entirety of myself with anyone other than him. Life gets so busy; it's easy to get hung up on just talking business, "What's for dinner?" "What time is the game?" "What's the schedule for tomorrow?" The conversations between husband and wife that build intimacy are the ones that reveal the heart or fuel the mind.

Sex. Yes, sex is the third way we build intimacy. This topic could use an entire book. There is so much to be said about sex in marriage, but all I want to say about it here in this context is that a couple who is pouring their lives into a family and ministry need to have sex often with each other. Unlike any other thing, sex has the potential to bring two people closer and more intimate. It's the physical joining of two people. It's part of the sacrament.

The juggling game of Chris's travel schedule, family life, and NFP was a crazy storm for many years. I will not pretend otherwise. Again, this requires a lot more than just a few lines, but no matter how arduous things got, we both felt that keeping the physical side of our relationship healthy was of utmost importance. It's not an accident that we have nine children.

In the end, working on building intimacy in your marriage will help keep sin at bay. The unitive power of a functioning marriage is the perfect antidote for the sin that lies in darkness.

The Three Tips

Maybe you find yourself a bit overwhelmed after reading through the obstacles many in marriage and ministry face. If so, know that you are not alone. We too have struggled to find balance. But, this book isn't just about identifying those struggles and obstacles; we also want to extend a helping hand by giving you a few tips. When we look over the whole of our marriage and assess the ups and downs, we see three major factors that have contributed to its overall success.

These three tips apply to the comprehensive reality of your marriage. If these points are kept in the forefront of your mind and discussed on a regular basis, you will find that they will become so engrained in your relationship that you hardly notice them anymore. That is why we had to take a serious evaluation of our marriage in order to find them. These tips are just a part of us, and we want them to become a part of you.

In order to find a balance in marriage and ministry, you must be free to fail, focus on your individual faith journey, and be comfortable with the uniqueness of your situation. This is our final cheerleading chant for you. This life is a hard one; however, it is also a life filled with adventure, exhilaration, and intimacy with the suffering Christ.

Tip #1
Individual
Faith Life

Chris:

You can't give what you don't have. I think about this a lot when it comes to ministry. A long time ago, I began to do solo events outside of the band, and those presentations began to go so well that places would have me come back the following year. Some places would have me a few times a year. I was aware that I couldn't give the same talk to the same group each time so I began to develop a number of different presentations that would allow for me to come to the same venue repeatedly without doubling up on content. I had heard complaints from hosts bringing in presenters or artists that they could almost give the exact presentation of a particular minister because they never changed. It isn't as if they were mad that certain stories were repeated; rather, they just were amazed that nothing would change in the presentation. As I began to do more and more repeat business, I was very sensitive to what I'd heard and learned how to add stories and modify ideas to fit not only a group I'd seen before, but eventually to mess with my presentations so much that I could hit any group I faced. I remember one time doing a ten-day stint in the East. I was the speaker, and there was a band traveling with me from Church to Church. I made it my goal to give a different presentation every day, regardless of the amount of talks expected of me in that time, because I wanted the band to be fed and encouraged as well. It was an amazing trip and nice to know I had something to give a band who had likely heard it all a million times.

What I realized was if I was growing in my faith, I would be able to give my audience something current and relatable. I was asking real honest questions about my actions and beliefs, and that gave me relevant content. So, how do I continue to grow in my faith? It is very simple:

1. I need Jesus. I still need Jesus. I am aware of this every time I stumble and fall, every time I try and make things happen with little to no effect, and every time I am faced with something bigger than my skill set to handle. I need Jesus to help me because I am so prone to wrecking myself. I remember hearing a quote by St. Philip Neri, "Lord, be with me today or I will betray you." I have found such consolation in knowing that

the great saints were aware of their propensity to sin. I will always need Jesus, and he is never upset with that fact.

2. I keep asking why: Why did I say or do something? Why am I irritated or elated by another thing? Why. When I allow myself to ask why, I allow myself to learn. There is a reason I am doing a certain thing and a reason I am not. When I am honest in the answer to this question, I am growing. When I am growing, I have something to give to others who can likely relate. Why? Because we are all far more similar than we would often like to admit.

3. Align myself with grace: I realized a long time ago that I need grace. We are the recipients of grace by two primary means. The first is through prayer. Prayer opens us up to the grace given from God to act in a way that is fitting for our call as followers of Jesus. Grace is unmerited favor that God extends to us, but it is also that desire to do something different. That desire for change is given by God. When we pray and ask for help to do the good, we want to do, it is grace that assists us to sanctity. When we sin we lack grace. Prayer is general in its application of grace. It can

come and enable us to live as followers of Christ. The Second way we receive grace is the sacraments. The sacraments are specific in their application of grace. We receive the ability to live more like Christ from graces given in these sacraments. If we are thirsty and are drinking from a fountain that constantly flows, the water from that fountain is grace and we are able to receive it anytime we wish to avail ourselves of it.

4. Because I am filled with grace I can make the right decision, or the good, which will help me be the saint I am called to be. When it comes to my individual faith life, it ultimately isn't just for me. Obviously, I am praying that the way I live impacts those around me with a love that points them to Jesus. I will not be able to give to others if I have not received grace. However, Just because you receive grace doesn't mean you automatically forward it on to others in the way you treat them. You can easily receive grace and remain indifferent to those around you. Think of those people who pass the wounded man along the side of the road in the story of the Good Samaritan. Learned and religious men did nothing. Or think of the people who go to daily mass but give you the evil eye because your

child makes a noise. They are certainly receiving graces but not acting accordingly. With the grace I receive, I am now able to act in a way that is beautiful, whether I feel able to or not. Since grace is real, and I have really received it through prayer or sacraments, I can now truly act in a way that will bless others regardless of a feeling. For me to give, I have to receive grace and I have to act on it!

5. Make your faith life your own. We all learn and process information differently. What works for you? For me, I go through waves of certain things that really fill and motivate me. What motivates you?

I suggest finding and focusing on things that make you move, allow you to be filled, and bring you peace and joy.

1. Move: What I find is that stories give me the proper perspective to believe that I can do impossible things as well. When I hear about a person who asked God for the miraculous and it happens, I now want to do that, and believe God can because he has done so before. I am motivated by the way God works in others and know that he will do so in me if I ask. I can fall

and even fail, but if I am moving I will be unstoppable. What makes you move or do something?

2. Filled: What fills you? For me, I am often filled by listening to worship music. It can have a real effect on my actions and even thought process. When I was in college I remember one time listening to worship music when I fell asleep, and when I awoke, the songs were still playing in my mind so loud I thought the tape was still running. It was a very cool moment for me, and I realized that if I put good things in my mind spiritually I would reap the results. I also realized that the Scriptures were very important for my fulfillment. I read the Bible a lot, but I also memorized verses, prayed those verses, and would spend time sharing what I'd learn with friends. The sharing with others took the info I was thinking about and put flesh on it for my real life experiences. Find some good people to just share what God is talking to you about.

3. Peace/Joy: In the end, you can't keep doing something you hate. You have to find a way to walk and be in peace and in the things that bring you joy because that is what will sustain you and keep you moving in times of difficulty. While ministry and marriage are never

easy, working on growing in peace and joy within the sacrament and ministry are key components for success in both. I find that when I am feeling tension or a lack of peace, it is a sign that I am possibly heading in a direction that is not in line with what God wants.

Ultimately, you have a lot of freedom to explore what works for you when it comes to spiritual growth. You need to grow so that you have something to give to your family and those to whom you minister. I am often amazed at the lack of spiritual care ministers have for themselves. Recently a friend shared that he spent his entire adult life ministering to others, but he had neglected himself physically so much he was now reaping the unfortunate rewards. When it comes to personal growth you need to keep the physical and emotional alongside the spiritual. You can't love and minister to those in your family or community if you are a psychological and emotional wreck with a body that is failing. I am not talking about the beauty of redemptive suffering. You can keep going if you take care of yourself. You can keep giving in ministry and family life if you keep growing spiritually. You can keep going if you ask why!

Linda:

Chris and I became Catholic in 1999. This was a difficult journey for both of us. We spent at least a year reading, studying, and listening to tapes about every aspect of the faith. I had this deep conviction inside that drove me to learn for myself. Even though Chris was always the person who enjoyed reading theology books and had majored in Biblical studies in college, I needed to be able to defend our decision on my own. Being that conflict and objections were expected, I didn't want to respond with a blank stare when I was asked a question about our reasons. I remember saying that if Chris were to die, I wanted to be so convinced that I would remain Catholic, even without his strength of belief as a support.

Throughout our entire relationship, we have both placed our faith life first, even over each other. Of course, the road of spiritual growth is bumpy and not a continual upward trajectory. There have been times when one of us was stronger than the other; however, the beauty of a couple being unified in their faith is that when one is down, the other is there to lift them up. Honestly, I don't understand how a marriage survives a vast difference in faith, especially a marriage that is involved in ministry.

Now this may sound harsh, but I want to speak clearly. If one of the two partners in a marriage is in opposition to or not in full support of the other's religious beliefs, I feel that ministry should be taken off the table, at least for a time. In the end, if you have to choose between ministry and marriage, marriage should ALWAYS win. If your faith or calling becomes an issue in your marriage, God will never ask you to sacrifice your primary vocation for a secondary one.

I know; I see them too. There are plenty of examples of people in ministry whose spouse is not at the same level of spiritually. But if we look closely, the majority of those examples have marriages that seriously struggle or have ended in divorce. I've witnessed so many of these scenarios that I have lost count. I understand the dilemma. For many of these ministers, they lose their main source of income if they walk away from ministry. They have spent decades building their success. In some cases, the fault of the failure in their marriage doesn't rest with them.

God uses broken people. I can firmly attest to that truth. So I am not saying that a marriage has to be perfect or that the two individuals need to be spiritual giants; however, having a unified spiritual compatibility is crucial to withstand the onslaught of mess that becomes a reality when a person gives their life to the service of God.

The place to begin is with simply being on the same page. After that, I have three considerations for you that will help foster individual spiritual growth in each partner.

1. Encourage any positive step your spouse takes in the right direction. Expecting perfection or immediate growth will cause a rift in your marriage. We all struggle with wanting instantaneous results; however patience and encouragement is necessary. No one wants to be continually criticized. When positive steps are taken, recognize the effort. Be careful not to sound like an obnoxious arrogant spiritual bully though. Spiritual pride is disgusting. If you feel like the progress is too slow, ask the Lord to show you his heart on the matter. His patience with us is never ending. Allow him to fill you with mercy and love for your struggling spouse.

2. Set aside time specifically designated for praying as a couple. I understand the hesitancy to pray together. It can make us feel vulnerable. We are opening up the deepest parts of our heart. Yet that is exactly why praying as partners should be a component in your marriage. May I suggest that this time need not to be daily. Even if you manage once a week or twice a month, the benefits will be experienced. Along with prayer, include time for sharing with each other what you have been hearing from God in your own private moments. Whenever Chris shares his prayer experiences with me, I always feel encouraged, and I walk away having learned something new about God and about Chris.

3. This third point flows naturally from the last. Be open and vulnerable about your struggles and questions of faith. If I hold back and refuse to share my real and honest thoughts, how will I receive answers for them? Furthermore, I am hiding a side of me from my most intimate friend, my spouse. Allowing your spouse to ask those hard questions is promoting spiritual growth in them. Doubt, confusion, and lack of faith does not mean they are turning their backs on God; in fact, I see

them as positive signs of a desire to go deeper. Wrestling with truth is not the same as denying the truth. Your marriage should be a safe place for that wrestling to occur.

Allow me to reiterate. I am so grateful that the Lord uses imperfect people like me. He has been merciful to use our marriage and family despite how messy we are. The truth is that our messiness and imperfection is precisely the reason having an individual faith life is crucial to success of balancing the union of marriage and ministry. Keep striving for that growth, both in yourself and in the life of your spouse.

Tip #2

Free to Fail

Chris:

You are absolutely free to fail! I am confident you've not heard this from anyone employing you to do ministry. It is possible that you placed yourself under undo pressure, wanting to impress those who gave you the chance to minister, but honestly, you need to know that it is okay to fail. In fact, I would say it is necessary to fail in order to be successful. There are usually two approaches people take when they think of failure.

The first is deny and deflect. They take a lesson from our first parent and try and blame someone else for the reasons they have failed, or they don't acknowledge that what they have done falls into the fail category. This didn't work back in the Garden of Eden, and it won't work with you now. You need to realize that you are always going to need to grow and adapt when it comes to ministry. Denial and deflection just keeps you in a place that is less than excellent. When you remain in a place of mediocrity, it benefits no one—not you nor the ones you to whom you are ministering.

The second approach people take when they think of failure is defeat and despair. When someone experiences defeat they either learn from it, adapt and move forward, or they give in to despair. When a person gives in to despair after they have fallen short, it is like ink in water; it spreads and taints the whole glass. Despair feeds upon itself, and I can guarantee that the next time you try and do something in ministry you will look with an almost eager expectation for the sign that it is failing. It is as if we assume we cannot have success and so to avoid the pain of being hurt again, we allow despair to be our teacher, convinced that we will always be second best or worse.

Failure is often seen as the worst thing that can happen to a person in a particular career, including ministry. We approach ministry under the assumption that the same rules the world uses are the same rules in ministry. This is absolutely not true. In a secular job you will be penalized if you fall short of your job's expectations, and if underperforming occurs often enough, you could have a financial penalty or even be fired. It is all about productivity. Success in the work place can at times be heartless, reduced to bottom line results, and these qualities can even be found in ministry settings. But think about this perspective when it comes to marriage. You don't give up on your spouse because they didn't perform their job at an excellent level that particular quarter. If they didn't cook your meal correctly you don't give them a warning and threaten to replace them. If your spouse doesn't pick up the right ingredients from the store you don't threaten them with divorce. It seems ludicrous from this perspective, but when it comes to God calling you to ministry you are not 'called' or 'dismissed' based upon a level of productivity.

Ministry is a call from God, not conditioned on a particular place you live this out. If you are dismissed by one parish and move to a different parish, does that mean you are no longer called to ministry? No, and here is why: A person didn't call you to minister; God did. In a similar way, you don't give up on your spouse because things are difficult that month or even that year. A relationship that is grounded in commitment will work tenaciously to find ways to better their situation, not abandon ship because things are difficult.

Failure is advantageous because of a several reasons.

First, you now know through failure that a particular avenue was not effective when it came to the results you wanted.

Second, you have to remember that God is working sanctity in you along the way, and so appearances can be deceptive.

Third, you don't know what spiritual forces are working against you so don't assume that you have somehow "done" something wrong.

Fourth, it is possible that you need to try one more time before a break through occurs, and giving up is exactly what the enemy wants you to do.

Fifth, you only fail if you give up when God is asking you to continue. You don't fail because you stumble, fall, or are not successful. That is called life.

There is a story in the Bible that brings this home for me. It is the story of the talents. The master is going away and he gives to his servants money that they can invest while he is gone. One of the amazing parts of this passage is the phrase, "each according to his ability." The master knew exactly what each was capable of doing in the time he was gone, and so we could easily argue that the master is setting these servants up for success. We can also see that at the end of the story, for those who invest what they've been given, they are all invited into the same reward. Finally, we can at least acknowledge that those talents are all "gifts." Not one thing was done to deserve or earn that which they had been given.

So, oddly enough if you think about this story with ministry, it would be easy to assume that, here is a story that proves productivity is key and failure is not an option, but I think a bit differently.

The servant who has one talent and is confronted by the master says that he knew the master to be a hard man. I wonder who told him that? We can argue that the master is a generous man. He gives to each according to their talent and then wants to reward them for doing the best they can. This servant buries his talent and assumes the master is hard and so will risk nothing because of fear. He gives back the talent, unused, uninvested, and assumes that stasis and complacency will keep him from being reproved. The master is angry because even the most unaware person would know that putting the money in a bank to get minimal interest would have been better than burring the talent. Fear makes people do crazy and illogical things, but the master gives us an insight about the servant when he calls him wicked and slothful. Think about this, the master knew those were qualities of the servant, and I am assuming that is partly why he got one talent. It is almost like the master is saying, just one talent, surely you can do something with one. But the fear allows slothfulness to breed, and the wickedness of the servant causes him to think complacency is better than trying and failing.

When I speak about this passage of scripture, I ask people what they think the master would say if the servant with one talent said that he went out and tried to invest but eventually he lost the money. Every person who I ask, says they think the master would forgive the servant. See, everything they received was complete gift. They were free to fail because they did nothing to earn what they received in the first place. The trying is the key.

Another point worth mentioning is that the amount of time the master was gone was the amount of time needed for each servant to double their money. What we don't hear about is the process of each servant as they invested the talent during the time they had before the master's return. I imagine that those servants who had many talents failed a number of times along the way. There were times when they invested and lost, but they kept at it, trying and learning from their mistakes. We assume that the investment by these servants was one and done and they automatically doubled their money. The trial and failure along the way was their key to true success.

This is the secret for a successful marriage and ministry. In my twenty-five years of ministry I have failed a number of times. I have forgotten lyrics, sang off pitch, said the wrong thing, taken wrong turns, gotten into debt when I shouldn't have, put ministry before family, and any number of other things, but I never gave up. We never gave up. Linda and I would be tenacious in our desire to try and fail, try again and find what worked for us, and that is one of the most important tips in having a successful marriage and ministry.

It is easy to quit and give up, but you have been given much and are free to fail and try again. You are free to try and try, fall and stumble, and try some more until the day that Jesus takes you home, but you are not free to quit and bury your talents in the sand, assuming that God will just use that one person who has seemingly better gifts and talents. Did the person with a couple talents not try because the one with five talents could just do all the work? No. Each had a job to do with the talents they were given, and each was set up for success. Don't quit, my friends, because it is possible that the breakthrough you look for is just around the corner.

Linda:

One of my favorite stories to tell is about the time Chris and I moved to Grand Junction, Colorado, for two weeks. That's right, we moved there for two weeks, not visited or vacationed, we MOVED there with a car filled to the brim and not planning on returning to Florida.

We had been married for less than a year, I had just graduated college, our first daughter was on her way, and we felt stuck. We were living in West Palm Beach, Florida, and Chris had dropped out of college to work full time. We were unhappy with our situation and wanted a change.

Some very good friends of ours were from Colorado and had decided to move back. They had a dream to start a youth camp in the mountains of Grand Junction. Chris and I felt inspired by their vision. We saw it as a solution to our unsettled feeling and decided to join them in their move. So, we got out of our lease, gave away as much of our stuff as possible, moved the rest of it into Chris's mom's garage, and set out for our cross country drive in the dead of winter. Our poor parents were probably completely freaked out.

Looking back, we can see all the hurdles that the Lord put in our path that we jumped right over in our determination for change. I clearly remember coming down from the mountain tops of the Rockies and seeing Grand Junction spread out in front of me and knowing, really knowing in my heart, that we were NOT supposed to be there.

In the two weeks of being Colorado residents, we lived with our friend's parents, searched tirelessly for a job, walked the mall starving for the food we could smell but not afford, and went to a Don Francisco concert. That concert changed our lives.

It was during that concert that Chris heard the voice of God tell him, "What are you doing here? I didn't create you to run a youth camp. I created you to do what that guy is doing on stage."

The next day, we begged our family to send us money for gas, and we drove back across the country.

I take pride in that failure. It didn't ruin us. I can't even say we fully learned from it either. Yet, it was a great experience and an even better story.

If you embrace the idea that you are free to fail, you will live a more full life. Our lives are not meant to be puzzles that we are to decipher; rather, they are adventures we are meant to create. Sometimes, failure is a part of that story.

When it comes to marriage and ministry, give yourselves the freedom to be wrong. It's okay to change your mind. It's okay to make mistakes, even the ones that cost you. If the two of you are united in this calling of serving God, you can handle the bumps and bruises along the way.

Too often, we view failure as a sign that we are on the wrong track. If things get rough, it must be God telling us to turn around. But for me, it wasn't the difficult circumstances that led up to the Colorado move that told me we were wrong; it was my heart. Being that I really and truly wanted to do the will of God, his voice eventually broke through. We weren't living in rebellion; we were just misled. The Holy Spirit wants to lead us. He wants us to follow the will of God. It's a comfort to me to know that even when I am way off, he will gently, or not so gently, bring me back. That's the beauty of failure, it helps to assess and possibly recalculate your direction.

Our move to Syracuse, New York, a few years ago was a completely different scenario. We had hurdle after hurdle thrown at us, but this time, we could clearly see them. It was the most emotionally and spiritually draining nine months of my life. Both of us struggled with anger at God. We couldn't understand what he was doing. We surrendered our dreams over and over. However, all along we felt the gentle leading towards New York. It was incredibly scary to put so much hope and desire into something that could possibly fall apart, but we felt there was no choice. While the circumstances were saying the opposite of our desires, while our hope was being brought to its lowest points, and while our minds where going in circles with confusion, we had to keep walking forward. Failure was constantly on our minds. Even though the falling through of our plans to move wouldn't mean complete ruin for us, it would mean emotional bankruptcy. We had invested everything into it because that is where we felt led. It didn't make sense, but we stepped forward in faith knowing that failure would hurt like heck.

That is the reality of a life called to marriage and ministry. It's not a road paved smoothly or clearly lit. It can be dark, bumpy, and even treacherous. Faith in the Lord and faith in your mutual calling is what will keep you afloat during those difficult times.

Allowing failure to be a family friend is necessary. Without failure as a friend, fear will hold you back. Fear will control your decisions and manipulate your reality. Failure can be embarrassing, confusing, and down right painful; however, it's better than regret or being stagnate. Stick together and fail together. In the end, you will have the greatest stories to tell.

Tip #3

Be Saint You

Chris:

I think one of the most difficult, but certainly most rewarding, parts of my ministry journey has been learning how to be entirely myself amidst a sea of incredible ministers. This has been a long journey of trying to be comfortable in my own ministerial skin, but it is a journey, I hope, you can all undertake.

It's difficult to admit to myself, or say publicly, that I have felt in competition with another minister or ministry, but in a brutal attempt at honesty, I have. I can remember thinking at certain festivals where our band was performing that we were about to crush it when we got on the stage. I knew that we would lovingly destroy all others because we offered something that no other group had: awesomeness. Sometimes it was an antsy itch to be able to get on stage because I knew that the audience was ready to go to the next level, and it was like having teeth pulled sitting there waiting for the intro act to finish. It's hard to admit it but it is true. As I got older and started doing speaking, I really began to understand and see the beauty of working as a team. In a way, I had a bit of an insight into that having been a part of a band, but when you are on your own, there is no one else to blame if things fall apart. Working in a team you can see a ton of various personalities trying to figure out how to labor together, and that can be a beautiful dance or a fast track trip to the pits of hell. One of the things I realized in the team dynamic was that, while I may be able to do most of the things others were hired to do, I was in fact there to do just one specific job. This gave me a lot of freedom to relax and focus on the role I was invited to do. I began to cherish the beauty of leaning upon one another during a ministry weekend, knowing that I didn't have to carry the whole show. This is a lesson I have cherished and still find helpful to this day. Whenever I am leading a team ministry event I try to emphasize this point, because it is very difficult for people to actually believe. An example of this is when I see speakers come in and, in their allotted thirty-minute time slot, they spend ten minutes of it doing a silly game or something they would do when they are by themselves trying to win over an audience. In a team, that work has already been done, so the ten-minute game time is really just a waste of the time given for serious work.

Being in a team can change the whole dynamic of a ministry event, but only if you play your part and stop thinking you have to do it all.

One day I was about to give a major presentation, and I was with a number of other known Catholic speakers. My job was to crush the Saturday night talk, and I have to say I was ready to go. I remember seeing a fellow speaker leaning back with arms folded in his metal chair, looking as if he was ready to settle in for a long nap. I was a little miffed and wondered what he was doing because, honestly, I knew I wasn't a speaker people normally slept through. So, I asked him why he was so relaxed. He looked at me and said, "Chris, I'm just settling in and leaning back to enjoy the amazing job you are going to do tonight!" It kind of threw me. I thought he was showing disinterest, but he was actually settling in to be not only ministered to, but also to be amazed. It completely disarmed me. I wasn't feeling any competition, but in that moment, whatever subtle remnants were there, suddenly left. I was in fact empowered because I realized that this famous speaker wanted me to knock the talk out of the park. He was so invested in me that he wanted to sit back and be blessed. I am so thankful for him to this day for showing me the power of believing in one another. That night I remember feeling so excited and encouraged by this friend that I prayed this prayer, "Lord, you made me this way. I am going to go up and give you the best talk I've ever given." It was awesome.

Over the years, I have learned that I can't be anyone else but myself. When it comes to ministry, I can absolutely get better, but I can't be great if I am not myself. If truth be told, I could have learned this lesson from the relationship I have with my wife. Linda, doesn't like me because of what I may become, or because I am like someone else, she likes me for me. I am still a bit amazed by this, but she wants to be with me because, in fact, I am decidedly me. If I tried to be like anyone else in our relationship, I would rob the beauty of this union because I would be operating under the illusion of something I was not.

Recently I had the chance to talk with my childhood friend. He and his twin brother were instrumental in making my difficult childhood so much better. That day I chose to tell him how thankful I was for the role he and his brother played in my life. I said, "You know, when we were kids, I always felt like I needed you more than you needed me, but you were always so cool with it." And without skipping a beat, my friend said, "Chris, you made everything we did so much better." It was one of the most beautiful moments in my life. He liked me for me. I can remember trying to be like them so often, but being unable to do so. All of that trying was a useless attempt at wanting to belong. His comment made me realize, in fact, that I already belonged.

When I think about ministry, and even marriage, we could spend the whole time trying to be something that we are not, or we could just be ourselves. I have spoken a bit about this idealized version of ourselves, and want you to know that if you don't rid yourself of that false status, you will waste valuable years of truly touching the lives of family and friends, as well as those to whom you minister. We need to somehow learn to be comfortable in our own skin, and honestly that isn't an easy thing to do.

We need you to be the saint you are called to be, and to be that saint, you have to be brutally honest about who you are. With all of your flaws and brokenness, your dents and weaknesses, you need to let God minister to that person and not an idealized version of that person. When God meets you exactly where you are, paralyzed on the side of the road, you can speak with a conviction of authenticity that God truly saves. It makes the idealized version pale in comparison. You must allow Jesus to love you in the now, in your mess, because that is how you become a saint. It seems so odd, and almost impossible that honesty in our brokenness would be a catalyst to sanctity, but it does, because you can finally allow Jesus to minister to you. This will allow you to minister to others in a way that resonates with who they are beyond their false perspectives of holiness.

So many people I know look at their spiritual heroes and try to be like them. It would be like me trying to be another known speaker or musician. They are them, and I am me. We have to believe that God is capable of doing something extraordinary with us. You may feel your story to be bland and unimportant, but how powerful will his work in and through you be if you abandon yourself to seeing him love you and love through you?

We don't need another St. Augustine, Aquinas, Don Bosco, or Little Flower. We need a saint you, and that can only happen when you are willing to be honest about your need for a savior and your willingness to let him love you right where you are. I wonder what stories the wounded man told as he reflected upon the Good Samaritan and his generosity? Think of the woman at the well who told the story to her entire town of how Jesus told her everything about her life and somehow didn't condemn her. What did the woman caught in the act of adultery say as she went forth and sinned no more? We remember these people because their story of having encountered Christ in their brokenness and sin was so singular and beautiful that it was worthy of being remembered. So too you! Your story matters, but it has to be the real you.

If you have been married for more than a year, you know that there is nowhere to hide when it comes to a relationship. When you date you can give that smile, tell that joke, put on that charm, but in a relationship that is all in, you can't hide. I love that about marriage. You have to be yourself, and you have to really deal with issues because, in the end, there is nowhere to hide. Real love sees the mess and still chooses to love. Real love will work with the other to gain victory and become better.

Don't give up. If you find that you have compared yourself to others, that is normal. What we need though is for you to begin to realize that God is filled with joy at what you are doing because he made you in such a way that it is singular and unique.

St. Francis De Sales said, Be who God made you to be and be that perfectly well. What will it look like for you to be entirely you? It is likely the saint that we need now more than ever.

Linda:

After becoming Catholic in 1999, learning about the different saints was one of my favorite things to do. There are so many of them, and they all have amazing life stories and compelling journeys of faith. In some ways, these holy people are written about like they are super heroes. Some had super powers like bilocation, reading of souls, and floating in ecstasy. No wonder most of us believe sainthood as an unattainable. We are simply way too ordinary.

I am just a mom: changing diapers, cleaning up vomit, washing my "famous" husband's underwear, and falling asleep on the couch during family prayer. I don't have a "ministry." No one knows my name, except the school secretary, and to others, my spiritual gifts consist of feeding the masses with mac-n-cheese and pumping out babies every other year. Sainthood is reserved for those individuals who do God's work.

Ok, let's back up for a second. Why would anyone want to be a saint in the first place? Don't saints get killed? Don't they suffer horrible diseases or live in poverty? Some days it's hard enough just holding onto our faith or throwing up a few Hail Mary's. Making the extra effort to be a saint is just too much work. I have walked through trials that make me wonder why I ever wanted to be counted among these holy men and women. I don't think I have the fortitude for it.

The simple answer is because your version of holiness is needed. It's not just desired or valued; it's needed. Your holy life provides grace of which only you can give flesh and blood. The Church and your family depend on you. In this age of mediocrity, your radical commitment to love and service will stand as a light proclaiming the truth of the Gospel. We can no longer tolerate the status quo of spirituality. The extreme darkness of this time NEEDS extreme light: your light.

Now that you understand the importance of pursuing the initials ST. in front of your name, let's get back to the main point here: be saint you. God created you with unique gifts and skills. You carry burdens that others don't. Your perspective colors life's experiences with a shade that will help others see the truth more clearly. What you have, God wants to use in someone else's life. Therefore, if we were to spend our life trying to be like someone else, we will have done a huge disservice to the creative talents of God. He gave you your sense of humor, your attention to detail, your obsessive drive for order, your strength in the battle, or your gift for making the perfect chocolate chip cookie. He expects you to use them, not tweak them to match another person's gifts.

The way in which you use these gifts, the "job" you perform, is not what gives value to these gifts. For me, years and years were spent behind the scenes being the support for the work Chris was doing for the Kingdom. Yet, my gifts were still being used. They may not have been obvious to those outside the home, but if I had not been using my gifts, the whole of our marriage and ministry would have collapsed. I may not have seen it this clearly throughout those years, but once I started to emerge from the background and got put to work more in the public aspects of ministry, I came to see how my gifts had always been there. They weren't dormant; they were active. Even though my "job" in ministry was not always valued by others as significant, God saw the value.

Because these gifts were instilled in me from my Creator, they were as equally valuable as the work Chris was doing. The best part was that Chris saw the value in my calling as well.

If I've said it once, I've said it a million times, marriage and ministry is a calling for the insane. You have to be insanely committed and insanely supportive. The two of you have to lock arms in unity and be each other's biggest supporters. Giving value to the different expressions of each other's gifts, not minimizing them or comparing them, is of utmost importance. Washing the clothes for the trip is just as important as going on the trip. Providing the listening ear after a stressful event is just as important as running the event. Working from a dining room table is just as important as having a private office. You are in this together.

Being saint you necessitates that you know yourself. If you are unsure as to what gifts the creator has bestowed on you here are a couple tips.

Ask your spouse:

It was Chris's encouragement and insight that made

me realize that I have a calling to receive my certification in spiritual direction. We are often most critical of ourselves, so having your spouse give their honest and loving observations could be very beneficial.

Look to your past:

Take some time and reflect on your past. Look for those moments, even in your youth, where you excelled. Were there times when people showered you with complements? Was there a situation where you felt you came alive? You should be able to find a couple memories that stick out. Dissect those memories to see what strength or gift lies at the root of that experience.

Pray:

We will never fully know ourselves without taking the time to ask Jesus who we are to him. Get into the practice of contemplating God's love. Allow him to speak his heart to you. Don't approach it as a task to be completed; rather, settle in to a relationship of father and child.

My journey to know myself has been a great ride. The confidence I have gained, not only in my day-to-day existence, but in my life's calling in ministry, has reinforced the value of the talents God has given me. Not that I have arrived, or even have come close, but the pursuit of sainthood seems more possible. I don't have to try and be someone else. Jesus is happy with me, just as I am.

Conclusion

When I started to get really serious about my faith, I was all in, but I kept struggling with sin and a lack of perfection. I wanted God to see I was not going back to my past way of living, but that past was always nipping at my heals. What kept holding me back was this feeling that I'd been given a second chance, numerous second chances if you will, and I just felt like at some point Jesus would realize he'd picked a lemon. I mean, I could tell people who had addictions and were practicing horrible things—prostitutes, drug addicts, criminals, and the like—about a God that would forgive them because I believed that with every fiber in my being. But, to imagine Jesus would bless me, someone who knew the truth of Jesus' love but had failed, was very difficult to hold on to. The way that God loves us is not fickle nor is it conditional. That is so unlike what most of us have grown up experiencing and knowing. To let God love you, to be with him in a way that destroys past and inadequate thinking about love is part of the journey to sanctity. In the end, Jesus is so committed to you that he is all in even if you fully let him love you or not. Nothing can separate you from the love of God! Not even that thing you are thinking of right now. Let him love you, my friends. When that happens, you will be a better minister, spouse, and saint.

In many ways Linda and I could have reduced this entire book down to one main point: You and your spouse need to allow Jesus to love you more so that you can be a greater gift to one another and those to whom you minister. Do you want your marriage to thrive? Invite Jesus into your relationship even more. Do you want to grow in your faith and be a saint? Ask Jesus to help you realize how much he loves you so that you can have the proper motivation to "do" all you want to do for him. Do you want to have a thriving ministry? To be effective and productive? Remember you have been forgiven of your past sins by a God who is radically in love with you and even likes spending time with you. It always comes back to the truth of Jesus' love for you. I remember learning a song that articulated that truth as a small child. I would like to make it theologically correct if you'll indulge me.

"Jesus loves me this I know, for the Bible and Sacred Tradition tells me so. Little ones to him belong, they are weak, but he is strong. Yes, Jesus loves me. Yes, Jesus loves me. Yes, Jesus loves me, the Bible and Sacred Tradition tells me so."

Linda and I want to cheer you on. Let us know how we can bless you. You are not in this alone, and I can honestly say that we want to see your marriage and ministry thrive. We understand that there are a ton of factors and variables we were not able to address in this book, but you can always reach out to us and share a little of your story. We'd love to journey with you in any way we can. You can reach us by email: linda@catholicfam.org and chris@catholicfam.org, and we are not so famous that we have someone handle them for us. Let's keep in touch.

From our home to yours, our ministry to yours, and our hearts to yours know, that we pray for you find yourself closer to Jesus today than ever before. If you are struggling in your walk with Christ, we would love to help. I know that your broken heart will fit perfectly into the Sacred Heart of Jesus.

ABOUT THE AUTHORS

Chris and Linda Padgett live on a homestead in Central New York with numerous children, lots of animals and countless books. They love their life and feel blessed to be able to share their stories and heart with the world. This is their third book they have co authored, even though technically Linda should have received credit for every other book Chris put out because it would have been a catastrophe without her editorial eye. You can find more about the Padgetts by going to:

www.catholicfam.org, www.linda360.com

or www.chrispadgett.com

For bookings: chris@catholicfam.org

941-704-3394

CPSIA information can be obtained
at www.ICGtesting.com
Printed in the USA
LVHW080754100120
643081LV00020B/1905/P

9 780999 021132